Careers
in Counseling
and Human
Development

Brooke B. Collison, Ph.D. & Nancy J. Garfield, Ph.D.
Authors and Managing Editors

American Association for
Counseling and Development
5999 Stevenson Avenue, Alexandria, VA 22304

American Association for Counseling and Development
5999 Stevenson Avenue
Alexandria, VA 22304

Cover Design by Sarah Jane Valdez

WITHDRAW

Library of Congress Cataloging-in-Publication Data

American Association for Counseling and Development.
    Careers in counseling and human development /   edited by
    Brooke B. Collison, Nancy J. Garfield.
        p.   cm.
    Includes bibliographical references.
    ISBN 1-55620-072-2
    1. Counseling—Vocational guidance.   I. Collison, Brooke B.
II. Garfield, Nancy J.
BF637.C6C325   1990
361.3′23′02373—dc20

Printed in the United States of America

Contents

AUTHORS' NOTE vii

FOREWORD ix
Norman C. Gysbers

PART I: GETTING STARTED 1

CHAPTER 1: HOW TO USE THIS BOOK 3
Brooke B. Collison and Nancy J. Garfield

Work Settings; Moving Ahead.

CHAPTER 2: SO YOU THINK YOU WANT A CAREER IN
THE HELPING PROFESSIONS 7
Brooke B. Collison and Nancy J. Garfield

Counseling Careers; Human Development Careers; What Do
You Know About Yourself? Moving Ahead in This Book.

PART II: WORK SETTINGS 19

CHAPTER 3: CAREERS IN SCHOOL SETTINGS 21
Claire G. Cole

Where Do School Counselors Work? With Whom Do School
Counselors Work? Whom Do School Counselors Help? What
Does a School Counselor Do? What Are School Counselors
Like as People? How Much Money Do School Counselors
Make? How Do You Become a School Counselor? How Can
You Learn More About Being a School Counselor? What Is
the Future for School Counseling as a Career? Who Else Is a
Helping Professional in the School?

CHAPTER 4: CAREERS IN POSTSECONDARY SETTINGS ... 31
Susan R. Komives

Why Work in Postsecondary Education? Preparing for Student
Affairs Positions; Student Affairs Functions; Student Affairs
Careers—Academic Support Services and Academic Advis-
ing; Administration and Leadership of Student Affairs; Ad-
missions, Registration, and Enrollment Management; Athletics;
Career Development and Placement; Commuter Programs and
Off-Campus Housing; Counseling and Testing; Disabled Stu-
dent Services; Discipline and Judicial Programs; Experiential
Learning and Volunteerism; Financial Aid and Student Em-
ployment; Minority Student Services; Orientation and Entry
Services; Residence Life and Housing; Student Activities; Student Union Programming and Student Union Administration;
Involvement and Support. Recommended Readings.

CHAPTER 5: CONSULTING CAREERS IN COLLEGE
SETTINGS 49
Clyde A. Crego

Why Campus-Based Consultation? Types of Campus-Based
Consultation; Perparing to Be a Campus-Based Consultant;
Characteristics of Consulting Psychologists; Finding a Graduate Program; The Future of Campus-Based Consultants; Consulting to Off-Campus Institutions. References.

CHAPTER 6: CAREERS IN BUSINESS AND INDUSTRY 61
Bree Hayes

The Beginning of a New Era; EAP Counselors; EAP Administrators; EAP Professionals; Career Counselors; Outplacement Counselors; Employment Recruiters; Employment
Interviewers; Employee Services Managers; Equal Employment Opportunity (EEO) Managers; Training Specialists; Human Resources Managers; Organizational Consultants.
References.

CHAPTER 7: CAREERS IN PRIVATE PRACTICE 71
Burt Bertram

Structure of Private Practice; Focus of Practice; Counseling;
Consulting; Teaching-Training; Education-Certification-Li-
censing Requirements; Personal Characteristics; Income From
Private Practice; Is Private Practice for You? References.

CHAPTER 8: CAREERS IN PUBLIC AND PRIVATE
          AGENCIES 81
          Robert A. Male

Public Agencies: County Mental Health Programs; County
Youth Programs; Private Nonprofit Agencies: Family and Child
Services Agencies; Special Need Agencies and Programs; Private For-Profit Agencies.

CHAPTER 9: CAREERS IN FEDERAL AND STATE
          AGENCIES 91
          Andrew A. Helwig

Employment Counselor; Correction Psychologist and Correction Counselor; Youth Counselor; Parole Officer; Vocational
Rehabilitation Counselor; Military Counselor.

CHAPTER 10: CAREERS IN HEALTH CARE FACILITIES 105
           Joseph McCormack

Psychologist; Health Psychologist; Counselor; Therapists Using Artistic Media; Psychology Technician; Social Worker;
Nurse; Nurse's Aide/Psychiatric Aide; Rehabilitation Counselor; Occupational Therapist; Recreation Therapist; References.

CHAPTER 11: CAREERS IN RESIDENTIAL TREATMENT
           CENTERS 121
           Ross K. Lynch and Susan M. Wiegmann

Physical Therapist; Occupational Therapist; Speech-Language
Therapist; Psychologist; Recreation Therapist; Rehabilitation
Counselor; Vocational Rehabilitation Counselor; Behavioral
Specialist; Personal Adjustment Counselor; Case Manager;
Registered Nurse; Social Worker; References.

CHAPTER 12: CAREERS WORKING WITH SPECIAL
           POPULATIONS 129
           Barbara Brown Robinson

Multicultural Populations; Persons in Crisis; Aging Populations; Substance Abusers; Gender Issues; Health and Wellness;
Special Need Agencies.

PART III: MOVING AHEAD 139

CHAPTER 13: CREDENTIALING, CERTIFICATION, AND
            LICENSURE 141
            Judy Rosenbaum and Sharon J. Alexander

    Accreditation; Licensure; National Certification; Professional
    Associations; Accreditation and Certifying Bodies; Table 1—
    Key Factors in Credentialing.

CHAPTER 14: WHAT NEXT? 147
            Nancy J. Garfield and Brooke B. Collison

APPENDIX A: PROFESSIONAL ASSOCIATIONS, CERTIFY-
    ING GROUPS, ACCREDITING AGENCIES 151
APPENDIX B: MATRIX OF OCCUPATIONAL TITLES AND
    WORK SETTINGS 157
CONTRIBUTORS 163
INDEX OF OCCUPATIONAL TITLES USED IN THIS
    BOOK 167

AUTHORS' NOTE

This book began as an idea discussed among a group of people who wanted to ensure that individuals who were trying to decide what they would do with their lives would have information available on the many career opportunities in counseling and human development. The original ideas about the book took shape when thirteen people agreed to write chapters describing different work settings in which those careers could be found.

We want to thank the writers who described the career opportunities found in this book. They each said, in one way or another, that they hoped that their contribution would make the process of career decision making more effective for the readers who would be in a deciding stage.

We also want to thank the readers of this book. We hope that they will find something that will make their decision process better for them. We invite your commentary about that. We believe that good decisions require good information. We hope that the information you have here is good for you.

—Brooke B. Collison
Nancy J. Garfield

FOREWORD

Society is changing and the changes continue to accelerate. Our nation's economy is increasingly international in scope and structure. As a result, our nation's industries, occupations, and work force are changing. The family structure also is changing. Single parent families and blended families are becoming the rule rather than the exception. There is an expectation of lifelong learning. People are living longer. And, there is increasing concern about problems such as substance abuse, suicide, and sexual experimentation. These societal changes and problems are not abstractions. They are real and they are having a substantial impact on the growth and development of children, young people, and adults.

Why do I list these societal changes and problems? I list them because as we enter the 1990s, the need for highly qualified professionals in counseling and human development to assist individuals in dealing effectively with these changes and problems will increase, not decrease. It is clear that all individuals in our society, whatever their ages or circumstances, can benefit from the work of professionals in counseling and human development.

Perhaps you, too, are concerned about societal and individual conditions and concerns these changes and problems are causing and would like to consider becoming a qualified professional in counseling and human development work to help others deal effectively with these concerns. The problem is that you don't have enough information about these fields and the professionals who are involved, and whether or not you would have the interest or the ability to do the work they do. So you ask, "Why doesn't someone write a book that would help me consider what occupations are available in counseling and human development, and whether such work is for me?" Well, someone has. Brooke Collison and Nancy Garfield have written *Careers in Counseling and Human Development*. This excellent book will help you compare yourself with people in the field, provide you with information about the various work settings where counselors and human development specialists work, and assist you in developing a plan of action to become a professional in counseling and human development.

Use this book as a source of information for research and study. Use it often.

Norman C. Gysbers, PhD, NCC
Professor
Educational and Professional Psychology
University of Missouri-Columbia

Part I

GETTING STARTED

The first two chapters of this book tell you how to use the book to your best advantage. Chapter 1, "How to Use This Book," gives you an explanation about the three parts of the book and about the work setting chapters. Chapter 2, "So You Think You Want a Career in the Helping Professions," is an important chapter to study before you begin. In this chapter you will be asked to consider a number of questions before you make a career decision—especially one in the counseling and human development professions.

You will find a checklist in chapter 2 of questions to use as you work through the book. The questions in that checklist ask you to think seriously about yourself, your abilities, your interests, the sort of things that you do well and not so well, and include items that are important to consider in any job. It would be a good idea to make a copy of the checklist in chapter 2 and keep that at hand as you read other chapters.

1

Chapter 1

HOW TO USE THIS BOOK

Brooke B. Collison and Nancy J. Garfield

Many people would like to have a career in which they help others, but they may not know about the many occupations in the counseling, human development, and human services fields, nor do they understand the differences and similarities among those occupations. This book has been written to provide information about careers in the counseling and human development fields. Most of you know the school guidance counselor who assisted you in choosing classes for the next school year, helped you sort out a personal problem, or administered an interest inventory when you looked at possible career choices. In this book, we provide information about school counseling and many additional professions that enables you to work with clients to help them solve their problems.

This book is divided into three parts: "Getting Started," "Work Settings," and "Moving Ahead." The first part provides information about the general qualities of people in the counseling and human development fields: What are those people like and who are they? We will also discuss the types of educational programs one must attend to become a helping professional.

No two jobs are ever alike, even if they have the same occupational title. You may find that a description of an occupation in one chapter will differ from a description of that same occupation in another chapter—that is to be expected. In the same way, salary information may differ from chapter to chapter for the same occupational title. Keep those differences in mind as you read.

In part 2, "Work Settings," information is provided in separate chapters about 10 different work settings where helping professionals work. These are not the only work settings, but rather a representative sample of the major work setting options for counseling and human development professionals. For each chapter in part 2, the following questions will be answered:

- What are the types of places in which you might work?
- Who would you be helping?
- What job responsibilities would you have in this work setting?
- What personal characteristics do you need in order to work in this setting?
- As a new professional, what salary might you expect?
- What education and training do you need to enter these jobs?
- What credential or license is required to work in this setting?

Work Settings

Ten work settings are described:

Chapter 3: Careers in school settings. This chapter discusses the types of activities that school counselors do, such as providing one-to-one and group counseling for students, working with teachers to develop programs to improve the learning environment for students and teachers, teaching classes about subjects such as adjustment to school or career choice, or working with students about dealing with peer pressure. Several other careers in the helping professions that are frequently found in school settings are mentioned in the chapter.

Chapter 4: Careers in postsecondary settings. Colleges and universities, community colleges, and proprietary schools are all places where persons in the helping professions work. Careers in student services are described, such as orientation director, financial aids officer, residence hall complex coordinator, learning skills counselor, counseling center counselor, or student activities program coordinator. This is a long chapter because postsecondary education is a complex environment where many persons are employed in many different jobs.

Chapter 5: Consulting careers in college settings. Colleges and universities often use people from the helping professions in a consulting role. This chapter describes what that job is like and how one can become a consultant in higher education. Two ways to think about consultation are described in this chapter—consultation on your own campus and consultation to colleges or universities away from where you work most of the time. Campus consultation might be designed to help faculty and staff improve campus environments, help campus police improve their crisis management skills, help administrators resolve faculty conflicts, or help staff develop a program to reduce alcohol consumption at campus events. Other campus consultation jobs and skills also are described in this chapter.

Chapter 6: Careers in business and industry. There are a number of different counseling and human development positions in business and industrial settings. A new and growing occupation—employee assistance programs (EAP) consultant—is described in this chapter. Outplacement counselor, employment recruiter, training specialist, and substance abuse counselor are occupations included in this chapter. Common to all of these occupations is that the helping professional works in or with a business or industry.

Chapter 7: Careers in private practice. The chapter on private practice examines what type of person is well suited for a career as a private practitioner. In particular it addresses private practice activities that include one-to-one and group counseling, consulting, and teaching-training opportunities for private practitioners who are counselors, psychologists, and social workers. Private practitioners work for themselves or with other persons. It is a small business.

Chapter 8: Careers in public and private agencies. The public and private agencies (e.g., community mental health centers, social service agencies sponsored by religious groups, or special focus agencies operated by either public or private organizations) are places where many persons work who have careers in counseling and human development. Agencies often have teams of persons from several different professional backgrounds who work together.

Chapter 9: Careers in federal and state agencies. Agencies that are organized or funded by state or federal revenue are described in this chapter. The kinds of careers you will find in this chapter include counselors in the employment service, the military, or detention or correction facilities. Other counseling and human development careers in state and federal agencies include those of youth counselor, parole officer, vocational rehabilitation counselor, and correction psychologist. State and federal agencies employ persons in many different occupations.

Chapter 10: Careers in health care facilities. Nearly every community has some kind of health care facility. You will find a number of different careers in counseling and human development in the various kinds of health care facilities, including counselor, psychologist, health/ wellness counselor, social worker, music or art therapist, nurse, or aides in different specialties. This chapter describes many of those careers.

Chapter 11: Careers in residential treatment centers. Residential treatment centers are places where clients live during treatment. There are many different kinds of residential treatment centers, and each has opportunities for persons with education in the fields of counseling and human development. Recreation or physical therapist, rehabilitation counselor, speech-language therapist, psychologist, and case manager are a few of the occupational titles described in this chapter.

Chapter 12: Careers working with special populations. The last chapter in this section describes some of the helping occupations frequently found in agencies organized to respond to the needs of special populations. In this chapter, "special population" refers to any identifiable group of people with a need that is unique for that group. For example, homeless persons represent a "special population" with unique needs. Women who have been sexually assaulted would also be described as a special population. The counseling and human development careers in this chapter are found in agencies that respond to these two special populations as well as several other special groups.

Moving Ahead

The third part of the book describes some of the things you might want to check on or do after you have read the chapters in part 2 that interest you. Chapter 13 presents information about credentialing, certification, and licensure for professionals in counseling and human development. This is important information for you to have as you examine different schools you might want to attend. Professionals in counseling and human development are frequently licensed, registered, or certified. What would that mean for you?

Chapter 14 suggests some "next steps" for you. It helps you to determine how you might use the information the book contains, what sort of things you might ask a counselor about your own occupational choice. Additional resources you might check if you have found one or more occupations that interest you are included.

Careers in the counseling and human development professions can be rewarding and exciting. They can also be frustrating and discouraging. These occupations provide many opportunities for the professional to help others grow and change throughout their life span. Human services professionals are expected to continue to be in demand in the future. Particular demand areas include work with adults and aging people, consulting, work with outplacement and career changers, and many facets of mental health counseling. This book should help you learn more about some of these occupations and provide other sources of information for further research or study.

Chapter 2

SO YOU THINK YOU WANT A CAREER IN THE HELPING PROFESSIONS

Brooke B. Collison and Nancy J. Garfield

Do you think you might like a career in the field of counseling or human development? Have you known persons whose careers enable them to help people and have you thought that you might like to do the same thing? This book will show you some of the different careers and how you might enter a career in a work setting where you are able to work with and help people.

Before you examine different work settings and learn about the occupations in each of those settings, it would be helpful for you to think about yourself and be able to describe personal characteristics that would be important in making a decision about a career in counseling and human development. Even before that, it is important to say what we mean when we talk about *counseling and human development*.

Counseling Careers

Counseling careers include those professional occupations that have the word *counselor* in the job title. In general, they include occupations in which you help people in some way—either by working with them in individual sessions or in small groups. You might do that work in a private office or in one of several work settings—schools, colleges, public or private agencies, health care settings, or even in large or small companies. Some occupations in this career field may be performed by people with other titles—psychologist, social worker, therapist, or child development specialist. We will use the term *counseling careers* to include all these occupations because they have one thing in common—they all emphasize

7

working with people to assist them in some aspect of their life. People might need assistance with severe problems or with minor decisions; however, in each case, the counseling professional does something to assist them in their particular situation.

Human Development Careers

Another term used in this book is *human development*. Careers in human development include many different occupations in which the professional works with people, but the job title may not include words like "counselor," "psychologist," "social worker," or "therapist." Human development careers are more frequently found in large institutions such as schools or colleges where the professional would work with people with more normal, developmental issues. In these situations, people need help not so much with problems, but with everyday concerns that require some kind of professional assistance. If you read the chapter about careers in postsecondary educational settings, for example, you will see that some careers in college settings deal with financial aid, advising, housing, or job placement. These are careers in human development. Just as in counseling careers, persons in these settings work with people.

What Do You Know About Yourself?

Before you can decide what kind of profession you want to enter, you have to know a lot of things about yourself.

How well do you like working closely with people?

- Do you want to work with people as your major job activity?
- Do you like working with a wide range of people?

What about your own problems?

- How do you feel about being helped with your own problems?
- How do you feel about helping others with their problems?

What work activities do you desire?

- What kind of work activities do you think you would find exciting and rewarding?

- What kind of work activities do you think would really bore you or make you lose interest in your work?

What kind of student are you?

- If you were to make a list of your academic strengths and weaknesses, what would be on those two lists?
- How much education do you plan to acquire before you enter a career area?

Do you have role models?

- Do you know one or more persons who have a career in counseling or human development? Do you want to be like them? Why? In what ways are you alike?
- How extensive or how limited is your knowledge of the different careers available in the field of counseling and human development? Do you think you know enough to make a good choice among those careers?

Do you have decision-making skills?

- Do you believe that you have good decision-making skills that would enable you to make career plans and life choices with confidence?

Do you want to work with people? Occupations are often described in terms of whether the worker spends more time with "data, people, or things." Nearly all careers in counseling and human development emphasize working with people. The exceptions might be a few occupations where research or information is emphasized, but the ones described in this book will most commonly describe "working with people" as a core of the job to be performed. Do you really like to work with people?

That may sound strange, but it is presented as a serious question you must ask yourself in making a career decision. "Working with people" means that you would be in contact with people much of the time in your job—you would listen to them talk about themselves, you would hear them describe their problems, you would work with people who are upset, and you would spend time in conference with people whose lives might be unpleasant. The important question to ask yourself concerning work with people is, *"Do I like to be around all kinds of people and can I maintain interest in them?"* This is different than having many people around you who are interested in you.

Sometimes it is hard to find a good way to answer the question asked above. The question becomes even more complex when you ask yourself, *"WHY do I like to help people?"* If you find, for example, that you frequently spend time talking with your friends and that they often come to you with their problems, does that mean that you should enter a career in counseling or human development? The answer to that question may come in asking yourself, "Why do my friends come to me and what do I get from helping them with their problems?" If the answer is that they come to you because you tell them what they want to hear or because you will solve their problems for them, then a career in counseling or human development *may not* be a good choice. If you find that you like to have them bring their problems to you because it makes you feel important or it gives you some kind of power or control over them, then a career in counseling or human development *may not* be a good idea.

On the other hand, if people come to you because (a) you are a good listener, (b) you remain impartial and objective, and (c) you help them figure out what to do but you don't feel they should solve their problems exactly the same way you would, then a career in counseling or human development *might be* a good choice for you.

What about your own problems? Do you think that you have to be free of personal problems to enter a counseling or human development career? Or do you think that the only way to help people would be to have had a similar problem and have solved it yourself? Persons who are thinking about entering careers in counseling and human development frequently express each of these ideas. Neither of these statements is true about people who enter counseling and human development professions. You don't have to be problem-free in order to enter the helping professions, but you should not go into the counseling profession in order to straighten out your own life. As a helping professional it would be important to remember that:

- all people have problems;
- no two people have the same problems;
- counselors are people;
- counselors have problems;
- a counselor and a client might have similar but not identical problems; and
- counselors need help with their own problems in the same way that other people need help with theirs.

If people who enter careers in counseling and human development believe that they should not have problems or that they should not reveal their problems to other professionals, they are forcing themselves into an unhealthy situation. They are presuming to help others or to ask others to seek help when they are unwilling to do the same for themselves; therefore, we suggest that it is important for the counselor to be able to acknowledge that problems do exist and to be able to seek help for those problems. We are also saying that *it is not necessary* to have had a particular problem in order to help people with that problem.

You do not have to have been a child of an alcoholic family in order to help children of alcoholic families; you do not have to have been divorced to help people who are divorced; you don't have to have lost a parent in order to help others who have had a parent die. At the same time, *if* you *are* a child of an alcoholic family, you might have some insight into the concerns of persons from an alcoholic family, *but* their experiences are still different from your own, and to assume that they are the same is not a good basis for working with other people.

Another important issue to look at concerning the helping professions and your own problem history is connected to problem solutions. Sometimes a person who has solved a problem wants to become a helping professional so that everyone with a similar problem will adopt the same solution. Such people can become fanatical about having other people "do what they did" to stop smoking, to get off drugs, to make their marriage better, or to go to the same college that they attended. These are not good counseling approaches. They are *not* good reasons for going into the counseling or human development professions.

It is important to be willing to see yourself as human—that means having problems just like everyone else. It is important to be able to seek out and accept help with those problems. And it is important to find solutions to those problems. After all, if you enter one of the careers in counseling and human development, you will expect people to come to you with their problems, just as you should be able to take yours to someone else.

Rewarding work activities. Do you ever fantasize about an ideal job? Do you know what sort of things make you feel good about your work—whether at school, in a job, or at home? Do you need to see the results of your work in order to feel good about it, or can you work on a project and never know how it will come out, perhaps not even getting credit for your work even if it does work out well? Can you work in the background and enjoy the fruits of your labor, or do you have to be right out in front getting the applause?

In many careers in counseling and human development it is difficult to know if your work is successful. Sometimes your success may not be known for a long time—perhaps several years. There are instances where a person you might be working with will be successful, but you won't know whether their success was due to something you did or a combination of other factors. In addition, counselors work privately and confidentially with clients, and if success is achieved in some activity, clients aren't always likely to stand up and give credit to the counselor who helped them.

People change very slowly. Some problems that counselors and others work with are difficult to change. For example, people who work in prisons often talk about the "recidivism rate"—the rate at which persons who are released from jail return because they haven't changed behaviors. The same problems exist for counselors who work with alcohol or drug abusers—clients may complete a treatment program and seem to be "cured," but in a short time after their release or completion of the program, many may be using alcohol or drugs again. This can be discouraging for the counselors who work with such persons. Do you think that you would be able to feel good about your own work if the signs of success were few and far between? Could you have a sense of accomplishment or be satisfied with your job if only 1 out of 10 people you worked with was "successful"?

The rewarding side of a career in the counseling or human development field comes when you see a person you have worked with solve a personal problem, make a decision that you both know is a good one, or develop good feelings about themselves. When the person you have been working reaches a point where your services are no longer needed, it can be a good feeling—one that you will know about but may not be able to share with others. In many counseling situations, you may never know the outcome of your work.

Perhaps you might think about yourself in terms of *what you need in order to feel good about what you do.*

- Do you need to feel that you have done your job well, or is it more important to see the outcome of your job?
- Do you need to have someone notice your work and tell you how well you have done, or can you be satisfied knowing for yourself that you have done a good job?
- Can you be patient and wait for the outcome, or must you have the results immediately?
- Can you be satisfied with small steps toward a goal, or are you happy only when the final goal has been reached?
- Can you be content working in a situation where you cannot control the outcome, or must you be in control in order to feel good?

People are best suited for counseling and human development careers if they can be satisfied to (a) know they have done the best they can do, (b) judge their jobs for themselves, (c) be patient with outcomes, (d) be satisfied with small steps, and (e) be able to work in situations that they cannot control.

You also might think about the question: *What do you need in order to feel good about yourself?*

- How do you feel when you do and don't get praise or criticism?
- What do you do when you get tired or depressed?
- Do you have the kind of good habits that maintain your health— habits such as eating well, exercising, and finding variety in your daily life?

Do you have to earn a lot of money in a job to feel good about yourself? The income for occupations in counseling and human development can range from very low for part-time paraprofessionals to very high for highly skilled consultants or persons who have executive positions or responsibility. Most occupations in counseling and human development will pay moderate wages, and people who have a need for a high salary or income tend not to enter these occupations.

How do you react to the problems you encounter in your own life? Can you see them as situations that can be resolved to your advantage? Can you seek help with the problems you have? Do you have a circle of friends with whom you can share your concerns and from whom you know that you would get understanding and support? Do you have a good sense of your own values and beliefs and know enough about yourself that you could be confronted with conflicting values and not be upset? If you can answer ''Yes'' to the last four questions, you are a good candidate for a career in a counseling and human development profession.

Are you a good student? Nearly all careers in counseling and human development require undergraduate and graduate study. You will see in the chapters that follow that some careers demand more education than others, but graduate degrees are common for most. What kind of student are you? A majority of the coursework for careers in the helping professions will emphasize reading, writing, and verbal skills. In addition, specialized study in counseling and human development professions will include coursework in several of the behavioral sciences—psychology, sociology, or anthropology—as well as coursework in statistics and research methodology. Admission to graduate study for the majors in these fields will require good performance on undergraduate studies as well as having met other admission criteria.

The kind of academic courses that have high relevance to careers in counseling and human development are the language arts—written and oral expression; social and behavioral sciences; mathematics—especially statistics; and academic activities where you have social interaction with people. The academic emphasis would be on interactions with people, understanding people, and being able to feel confident about yourself in those interactions.

The amount of education required will depend on which career field you explore. You will find that you can enter some careers in counseling and human development with an undergraduate education. Most will require a graduate degree—at least a master's degree—and some will require a doctoral degree. Some careers in counseling and human development may require advanced training or an internship in addition to a doctoral degree. An internship may be necessary before or after completion of a degree, and will represent a significant amount of supervised time spent in professional work.

Who are your models? Do you know people who are professionals in one of the counseling or human development careers? Watching and talking with people can be helpful in learning what people do, how they got into their field, what they like and dislike about it, and whether they would enter the same field again if they had the opportunity to do so. Frequently, people may want to enter a field because they have been helped by a professional and they decide that they would like to be just like that person. This is not a bad reason for choosing a field if the other characteristics you know about yourself match those necessary for that career. Choosing a career just because you had a good experience with a particular counselor or advisor is not a good reason in itself to make such an important decision.

Another common reason people want to enter one of the helping professions is that they have or have had a particular problem or situation in their own life and they want to see other people solve it in a similar way. This is not a good reason for choosing a career unless you have truly worked through all the aspects of the problem issue, and you have other reasons for making that career choice.

It would be a good idea to know several persons in a profession before deciding that should be your own career. Knowing one professional person in a counseling or human development occupation provides a limited view of the career field.

Your career decision-making skills. How good are your own decision-making skills? There are few decisions that you will make in your life that are as significant as, "What are you going to do for your life's work?" If you have studied career decisions, you know that few people make *one* decision early in life and then enter an occupation and remain there until they retire. It is more likely that you will change your mind about what you are going to do several times before you actually enter your profession. After entering a profession, other kinds of changes may be natural or logical—changes such as advancement through the stages of a career in what might be called a "career ladder." Other career changes may be more unexpected, as you decide to leave a profession altogether and do something else with your life. Frequently, success in one area may lead to possibilities in a different occupation. Each of those changes is a critical point along the path of career development. Each requires critical decision-making ability.

How do you make decisions now? Do you gather information, consider alternatives, think about consequences, and then make careful steps toward implementation? Or do you listen to other people and try to do what they want you to do rather than what you would want yourself? Do you move quickly into new decisions without much thought of the past and the future, or do you take a long time to think and plan before you act?

It is important for you to spend some time thinking about your decision-making style and then apply that knowledge to make a career decision. Make a list of some of the major and minor decisions you have made in the past several years. After you have listed those decisions, think about how you made them. Apply the questions found above to the decisions you listed. How many of the decisions do you look back on as "good" decisions, and how many are decisions that you would like to have the opportunity to do over? Can you draw any conclusions from that about how you should look at decisions that are as important as entering a career in the counseling or human development professions, or in any other career area for that matter?

Moving Ahead in This Book

Are you ready to move ahead? Check off the items on the following list before you select one or more of the chapters to read:

Yes	No	Questions for Myself
—	—	Do I want to work with people as my major job activity?
—	—	Do I like different kinds of people?
—	—	Can I accept help from others for my own problems?
—	—	I like to help other people with their problems.
—	—	I would like to work in an office setting.
—	—	I would like to work alone.
—	—	I would like to work with a number of other people.
—	—	Written and verbal activities are interesting.

—	—	I am a good student, particularly in language arts and social and behavioral sciences.
—	—	I can describe my own academic strengths and weaknesses.
—	—	I plan to earn a college degree and have thought about going on to graduate school.
—	—	I know more than one person in the counseling or human development field.
—	—	I am able to make good decisions for myself.
—	—	I am not easily influenced by other people in the important decisions about myself and my career.

Keep the above checklist ready as you read the chapters that follow.

Title duplication and omissions. You will find that each of the chapters describes a different setting in which people in counseling and human development careers work. Some occupational titles, like *counselor*, may be found in several chapters; however, you will find that the description of "counselor" may be different from one setting to another, just as what a teacher would do in an elementary school is not the same as what a teacher would do in a high school, even though the title, "teacher," is the same in both. There are more occupational titles in any work setting than can be described in each chapter. For example, "consultants" may be found in nearly all work settings, but they are described only in five chapters. The matrix in the back of the book will show you which occupations are described in this book as well as additional work settings where those occupations are found.

Each chapter will explore job features, job descriptions, worker characteristics, salary information, education requirements, licensing, and certification of different occupations in different work settings. This should help you make comparisons about careers in different work settings, even if they have the same occupational title. Each chapter is complete in itself, so you can read some or all of them in order to answer questions about a specific occupation or a specific work setting.

Salaries. Note: Salary information for the same occupations may differ from chapter to chapter. This is not unusual. Several salary information sources have been used in this book, and you should check the current issue of the *Occupational Outlook Handbook* (usually identified as the OOH in this book) as well as local salary information to obtain the most current and accurate information for yourself.

Index. If you want to find all the places a single occupation has been mentioned (such as *counselor, dean*, or *consultant*), the index will give you that information.

When you have finished reading the work setting chapters, we suggest that you return to the above checklist one more time for a review. Then read chapter 14 called "Next Steps."

Good wishes to you.

Part II

WORK SETTINGS

There are 10 chapters in this section. Each chapter describes a work setting and careers in counseling and human development that might be found in the work settings described. The authors have given you a realistic look at different work settings; however, it is important to note that no two work settings are the same—even when they are called the same. For example, chapter 4 describes many different careers found in post-secondary education. Although there may be a person called a "counselor" in nearly every institution of higher education, what a counselor does in one 4-year college may be very different from what a counselor does in another 4-year college—even when their titles are the same.

Another difference you will note as you read chapters in part 2 is that salary figures may be different for the same occupation described in different work setting chapters. Using the example above, you should understand that what a counselor earns at one college may not be the same what a counselor would earn at a different college. You always need to explore salary and job description data for the specific place in which you are thinking about working. The chapter authors have given you accurate salary information, but it is general information and will vary from place to place. Gathering the specific information about local salary and job requirements is your responsibility.

Chapter 3

CAREERS IN SCHOOL SETTINGS

Claire G. Cole

WHOM would you talk to in a high school if you were 15 years old and you:

- are panic-stricken that you are pregnant?
- wonder how to study to become an osteopath?
- want to join the band but know your family doesn't have the money to pay for band trips?
- think your auto mechanics teacher is picking on you because you are the only girl in class?
- believe your best friend is becoming an alcoholic?
- worry that you might fail English and not graduate?
- want to attend a liberal arts college and study music but your father says all the men in his family always attend a military academy?
- have a chance at a prestigious academic scholarship and want help getting recommendations and writing an essay?
- cannot stand your biology teacher one minute longer?
- need a job but can't read the job application well enough to fill it out?
- feel angry because you are in a special education class and think everyone is laughing at you?

WHOM would you talk to in a middle school if you were 12 years old and you:

- are 3 inches shorter than everyone else in your class?
- think your best friends of last year are immature and silly but don't want to give them up and be friendless?
- worry that your parents are getting a divorce?
- worry you might have AIDS because you sat next to a boy who looks really sick?

21

- hate to go to gym class because everyone picks on you in the locker room?
- know that your best friend is shoplifiting?
- have heard your father say that you might have to move to another city soon?
- want to graduate from high school in 3 years instead of 4 and don't know if that's possible?
- love your clarinet and wonder if there's some summer camp in music you could attend?
- need to earn money for school clothes because your mother just lost her job?

WHOM would you talk to in an elementary school if you were 8 years old and you:

- feel sick to your stomach every morning before you go to school?
- want to be a professional football player but your mother won't let you go out for sandlot football?
- think writing stories is great and want to learn more about that?
- hate your brother because he's so mean to you?
- have a pain in your back where your father hit you when he came home drunk last night?
- are in one classroom this year and all your friends are in another?
- don't know how to make good grades like your parents want you to?

The answer to whom you would go to for help in finding answers to all these questions is THE SCHOOL COUNSELOR.

Where Do School Counselors Work?

School counselors work with students from about the ages of 4 through 18 in primary, elementary, intermediate, middle, junior high, and high schools. Occasionally counselors work with students younger than 4, such as in preschool and other programs for handicapped or at-risk children that may begin as early as 2 years of age. And sometimes they work with postgraduate students who are still attending high schools who are older than 18. The number of high school counselors increased significantly in the 1950s. Recently more counselors have been hired to work with middle- and junior high-school students. Now more counselors are being employed in elementary schools, although most elementary schools in the country still do not have counselors.

Most high schools and middle/junior high schools in this country have school counselors. To be accredited—that is, be recognized as good schools—high schools must provide counseling services. In some states the number of students one high school counselor can be assigned is suggested by the state. A ratio of 250:1 would mean that a counselor would be responsible for 250 students. Thus, a high school of 1,000 students would have four counselors. The number is usually higher for middle/junior high—perhaps 400:1— and for elementary—maybe 500:1. This means that middle or elementary school counselors are likely to have very high numbers of students assigned to them, making it more difficult for them to provide adequate services for their counselees.

There are also school counselors in some other countries, including Israel and Canada, but the school counselor is more of an American tradition than are other professionals in education. Counselors who want to work in another country often serve in Department of Defense schools operated for dependents of American military personnel.

School counselors usually have an office in the school building. Some elementary counselors have a room where groups of students come for different kinds of activities. Often a counseling office suite includes space for visitors to sit while they wait for the counselor, a secretary's work space, storage space (sometimes a vault) for records and other materials, and a conference room where groups of people can meet. Sometimes the office is near the principal's office in the administrative suite; it also may be located near the parts of the building where students are in class. If a school has separate areas or buildings for different grade levels, often there will be a counselor's office in each area, rather than all counselors' offices being clustered in one space in the school. In a very small school, a counselor might have only a desk in a shared office where he or she would work 1 or 2 days a week. Larger, more modern school buildings are likely to have counselors' offices spread throughout the building, rather than all in one place.

With Whom Do School Counselors Work?

School counselors are a part of the team of people working in the school. They work closely with teachers and administrators to help their counselees. Often elementary and middle school counselors teach guidance lessons in the classsroom, joining the regular classroom teacher in a team-teaching effort. Counselors consult with teachers when a particular student is having difficulty and often include parents in the consultation. School principals seek counselors' help to plan programs and to identify ways to improve the school so that students can learn better. Counselors also work with educational specialists: nurses, social workers, gifted specialists, homebound teachers, psychologists, special education personnel, and others who gain specific information about individual students from the school counselor.

Mental health professionals from the community often seek school counselors' views of their clients who are enrolled in schools. Permission, or at least notification of the parent or student, is required whenever information is shared with a substance abuse counselor, licensed professional counselor, psychiatrist, probation worker, social services worker, psychologist, or other mental health professional.

Whom Do School Counselors Help?

School counseling differs from many other mental health professions because school counselors work with the entire student population—a psychologically healthy group. They do not see only students with problems who need therapeutic counseling; rather, they provide counseling in education and careers for all students. They may also, through classroom guidance, provide information and a degree of counseling for all students on how students develop normally, describing some common feelings, worries, and fears that most students in an age group encounter. Although school counselors work with parents, teachers, and other adults who surround the student, the counselor's primary client is always the student. The school counselor is—first and foremost—a student advocate.

How students are assigned to counselors varies from school to school. Sometimes high school counselors are assigned to the same students for the students' entire high school career; the counselor begins with the group in 9th grade and "moves up" with their grade through the senior year, picking up a new group of 9th graders after the first group graduates in 4 years. Other counselors have one section of the alphabet; that is, they might have a group counseling session with all students in the first half of the alphabet, gaining new 9th graders each year and losing about one-fourth of their clientele each year as seniors graduate. In both of these assignment methods, the counselor remains with the students all 4 years in order to get to know them well. In other schools, counselors become specialists in knowledge about a particular grade level, with a counselor always having students in the same grade level each year. Thus, a student has a different counselor for the 9th, 10th, 11th, and 12th grade. The advantage to this method of assignment is that the counselor can become an expert in knowing about such senior concerns as how to get into college, what military requirements are, and other such things that students leaving high school need to know. The 9th grade counselor knows how to help people adjust to high school and lay out a plan for graduation. In yet other schools, a student may pick which counselor to see, with no method of assignment of students to counselors.

What Does a School Counselor Do?

A counselor's day in a high school can be very different from one in an elementary school, but all counselors do certain things, including:

- *Counsel with individuals or groups* of students who want to change some aspect of their behavior such as making better grades, getting along better with parents, making new friends, or other such topics.
- *Consult* with parents, teachers, principals, other mental health professionals, and others who deal with students.
- *Provide information* on a wide variety of topics, depending on the age of the counselees, from describing community helpers to kindergarten students to helping high school seniors understand the college application process.
- *Test and manage data* related to students. Usually counselors interpret tests and collect other kinds of information needed to help students do good planning and move to the next level of preparation for education and careers.

An elementary counselor's day might go something like this:

- Meet with parents and teacher about a new student before school.
- Visit three second-grade classrooms and conduct classroom guidance lessons on how to handle anger.
- Plan an open house program for parents with the principal and other teachers.
- Have a group counseling session for four fifth graders having trouble keeping friends.
- See three students by individual appointment who were referred by their teachers.
- Attend a staff meeting and help develop a specialized plan for a special education student needing counseling services.

Often an elementary counselor serves more than one school, so the schedule may be condensed while the counselor moves to another school around midday. Or the counselor may be in one school certain days of the week and in a different school on alternating days.

A middle school counselor's day might be a little different:

- Attend a parent conference with several sixth-grade team teachers before school.
- Supervise teacher advisory activity during homeroom period, when teachers deliver classroom group guidance to all students throughout the school.
- Counsel three individuals by appointment: one new student having trouble adjusting; one girl who has boyfriend problems; one boy who gets into fights.
- Conduct two group counseling sessions on growing into adolescence, which every seventh grader attends.
- Attend a seventh-grade team meeting to discuss students about whom teachers are worried.
- Meet with high school counselors to plan student orientation.

The high school counselor's day will be similar to the middle school counselor's, with a few different twists:

- Review all senior grade sheets to be sure everyone is in the right classes to graduate.
- Meet with a college representative who wants to leave information about her school.
- Counsel six students by appointment: college admissions questions, where to get a job, trouble getting along with a parent, fear of pregnancy, general unhappiness and lack of motivation, and schedule problem.
- Discuss with the principal plans for the annual College and Career Night.
- Arrange for a counseling group on substance abuse to be conducted by an outside agency.

All three counselors—elementary, middle, and high school—use the same skills of establishing a relationship with a student, identifying a problem or concern, planning ways to make changes in the student's way of behaving, evaluating progress, and following up with the student to be sure things continue to go well. But the topics and the techniques used vary greatly as counselors do different things in different ways with younger and older students.

What Are School Counselors Like as People?

School counselors like students and know how to talk to younger people. Not only must they have the skills of any other mental health professional, but they must also be able to establish rapport—to make students trust and believe in them—with young people. They typically have a genuine interest in students and are often the best adult "cheerleaders" students have. Usually one sees counselors at ball games, musical events, plays, and other places where their counselees are performing, because counselors like to see their students achieve. So they must be able to establish rapport and then have the counseling skills to help students achieve their goals. Counselors who work in schools must also be able to get along with adults, because they work on a team. Whereas a teacher may be able to work behind a closed classroom door, a counselor is in the mainstream of school life, working with virtually every individual in the building—both adult and student. Counselors must also be able to organize well, because they must see many students in a short period of time, return a seemingly infinite number of phone calls, and help plan many programs and activities. They must be ingenious thinkers because there are few rules for human behavior: Different solutions must be tried with different individuals. They must also have good judgment and common sense: As spokespersons for the school, they need to be correct and sensible. As observers of people, they must have a good understanding of human behavior and make good decisions: A missed cue may mean a suicide, a drug overdose, or a school dropout.

Because counselors are often called upon in a crisis, they must have a high energy level, be able to remain calm, and think quickly and clearly. If there is a suicide in a school, for example, a counselor must be able to function as a part of a crisis team without collapsing due to personal emotion. School counseling is a demanding but rewarding job for those who are able to work on a team, enjoy being around young people, and identify and use resources outside the school building.

How Much Money Do School Counselors Make?

Usually the pay for school counselors is based on a teacher's salary scale, although sometimes the director of counseling in a school is considered an administrator. Because they have master's degrees and often work more days than do teachers, they may have salary supplements that teachers often do not receive. There is a great range of teaching salaries within this country, but a beginning counselor with a master's degree can expect to earn more than $20,000 a year.

How Do You Become a School Counselor?

Most school counselors have been teachers before they became counselors, so most have an undergraduate (bachelor's degree) in a teaching area such as English, vocational education, elementary education, or some other subject. Teachers who want to be counselors usually enroll in a university program in school counseling that leads to a master's degree. The program of studies includes individual and group counseling theories and techniques; consultation; career and educational information; testing and measurement; working with special populations such as minorities, the gifted, and special education students; and other such courses. The program may also include coursework on working with families, substance abuse, and other special topics. Counselors do a practicum—supervised practice in a school working with an experienced school counselor—before they complete their work for a master's degree.

Usually there is specific coursework and practicum experience for the level at which the counselor will be endorsed to work—high, middle, or elementary school. Each state sets its own requirements for being a school counselor. If a person who wants to be a counselor meets those requirements, he or she is said to be "certified" or "endorsed" to be a school counselor.

It is likely that continuing coursework will be required to keep the endorsement up-to-date. The profession is constantly changing as people find new and better ways to help their counselees, and as new topics become important for counselors to understand. A few years ago, school counselors had no need to know about anorexia and AIDS; now they must understand both. Counselors also keep themselves up-to-date by reading journals such as *The School Counselor* and *Elementary School Guidance and Counseling* and by attending conferences sponsored by state and local branches of the American Association for Counseling and Development (AACD) and its affiliate for school counselors, the American School Counselor Association (ASCA).

How Can You Learn More About Being A School Counselor?

There are several good ways to learn more about school counseling.

1. A good source of information on school counseling are the counselors currently working in schools. They will be very happy to share their information with students who are interested in becoming school counselors, and they will know what is required in that state to be credentialed as a school counselor.
2. Another source of information is the *Occupational Outlook Handbook*, which is almost surely in the school guidance office. Other

similar publications give information on school counseling as a profession.

3. There may be a computerized career information service, such as the state's occupational information system, that is found in many school counseling offices or in some public libraries. Many computerized information services will give information on where to study counseling in a particular state and perhaps some employment outlook trends for that region.

4. Universities with a master's degree in counseling are another good source of information. Professors in counselor education can tell prospective students about what kind of preparation program is involved, as well as entrance requirements. They probably have thoughts on undergraduate preparation that could be helpful before undertaking graduate study in counseling.

5. Professional organizations such as AACD and ASCA have state and local affiliates. These organizations would welcome a student visitor who is a prospective counselor.

What Is the Future for School Counseling as a Career?

In most states, there seems to be a bright future for school counselors. Although there have been some cutbacks in school counseling programs due to reductions in funding for special services, most states are putting emphasis on the kinds of services school counselors offer. As more attention is paid to individuals through special education and programs for the gifted, more information and support are needed at the school level for students. Dropout intervention is a current concern for many educators and legislators; school counselors are likely to be involved in dropout programs. As American society believes in individual choice and has the affluence to provide the means to help individuals make wise choices, the school counselor will figure importantly in schools to help students see their options in life and plan programs to get them there. Societal concerns such as AIDS, substance abuse, minority concerns, and others mean that someone has to pay attention to the individual youth growing up—and often that "someone" is the school counselor.

Another important trend in school counseling is the emphasis on counseling for all students, including those at the middle and elementary school level. Increasingly, counselors are being added in those areas, making a whole new cadre of counselors necessary, just at a time many of the counselors trained in the 1950s and 1960s are entering retirement. Many schools rank counselors among those hard-to-find individuals who are very important to the smooth functioning of any school.

Who Else Is a Helping Professional in the School?

Many school principals and teachers have some training in basic counseling skills and are very willing and able to help students with their personal concerns. School psychologists and school social workers have training similar to that of school counselors, but have different responsibilities within the school system. Much of their time is spent with the evaluation required for students receiving special education services. The school psychologist is skilled in administering and interpreting tests, especially tests that measure characteristics related to students' success in school. They counsel parents, students, and teachers about factors that influence students' achievement. School psychologists often provide consultation for teachers regarding their students with learning or behavior problems, and some do individual or group counseling with students. Usually a school psychologist serves several schools, or may be a professional outside the school system hired specifically to do special psychological or educational evaluations.

The school social worker works between the school and the home to help students do well in school. Often the school social worker has responsibility for trying to get students to school when they are poor attenders. The social worker also helps families find the help they need from other social service agencies. Some social workers have a great deal of training in counseling, especially family counseling or therapy. Others have primarily attendance officer responsibilities. There are not as many regulations about the qualifications or case load for school social workers as there are for school counselors or school psychologists. Usually these professionals serve several schools within the school district; often their work is primarily with attendance problems or special education evaluations.

Further Information

Your school counselor or counselor at a career center can give you additional information about careers in school settings. The following associations can provide specific information also. Their addresses are in the appendix.

American School Counselor Association
American Association for Counseling and Development
American Psychological Association
National Association of School Psychologists
National Association of School Social Workers

Chapter 4

CAREERS IN POSTSECONDARY SETTINGS

Susan R. Komives

Introduction

American postsecondary education is a major employer of counseling and human development professionals. Approximately 40% of all college-age youth, more than 13 million students, are enrolled in over 3,200 accredited postsecondary institutions. Each of these institutions employs from 10 to 300 counseling and human development professionals. Postsecondary education is a big business.

Student affairs staff work with students individually, in groups, and in campus communities. They work in partnership with teaching faculty and other campus administrators to help students have a personally and academically successful college experience. Student affairs professionals are concerned with the development of the whole person. They are concerned with the intellectual, occupational, cultural, physical, emotional, social, and spiritual development of students and acknowledge the individual differences of each student due to such factors as their gender, sexual orientation, race, ethnicity, age, religion, abilities, and aspirations.

Student affairs professionals work hard to help students have a productive college experience and to achieve personal and academic success. These professionals work in areas that include admissions, career placement, personal counseling, student activities, religious services, and athletics. They help students living on campus and commuting to campus; provide services for special students such as those with specific disabilities; and provide programs for special groups: women, ethnic minority students, disabled students, and older adults. They educate students in leadership programs, campus activities, and cultural or recreational programs, and

31

hold students accountable to community standards through judicial systems. Student affairs professionals consult and collaborate with many other campus staff to help the campus be responsive to students. These professionals need skills such as counseling, advising, consulting, teaching, assessing, administering, researching, leading, managing, and programming.

Institutional Diversity

Postsecondary education is the broad name used for training and education beyond high school. American postsecondary education is diverse, including four categories of institutions:

- community and junior colleges;
- proprietary schools and technical institutes;
- four-year colleges; and
- universities.

Community or junior colleges are 2-year institutions offering associate of arts (AA) degrees and continuing education courses. They offer several educational choices including a college transfer track preparing students to go on to a 4-year degree; and a vocational/occupational training track preparing students for immediate jobs, such as air conditioning service technician, nurses aide, or dental technician. These colleges emphasize quality teaching and a concern for student growth and development, with an emphasis on the older adult learner. There are also some 2-year schools for upper-division students that begin enrollment of transfer students at the junior year. *Four year colleges* are often small (usually under 5,000 students) and usually focus on the liberal arts. Students enroll to earn a bachelor's degree and many pursue graduate study after graduation. *Universities* offer the BA and BS as well as some graduate degrees such as master's (MA, MS, MEd) and doctoral (PhD, EdD) degrees and various professional degrees such as Doctor of Medicine (MD). Universities generally value faculty research and the advancement of knowledge, and expect good teaching; they offer strong student affairs programs, yet their large size makes it hard to provide personal contact with each student. In addition, American postsecondary education includes as many as 8,000 *proprietary schools and technical institutes*. Proprietary schools are private, for-profit institutions that offer specialized training programs (such as culinary arts, computer repair, or cosmetology). Technical institutes are private or public, and focus on specialized skill training. They generally offer only basic student services.

Within each of the four categories is additional diversity. An institution may be primarily residential (students live on campus in residence halls), a commuter campus (students live at home or in apartments near campus); rural or urban; public or private; nonselective (many students who apply may be admitted) or very selective (a small proportion of applicants are admitted); religious or secular; primarily liberal arts or vocational; quite large (50,000 students) or very small (350 students); and financially healthy or financially struggling. Some colleges have a specific focus, for example, military schools, women's colleges, historically Black colleges, or seminaries. The characteristics of each college and the mission of that college create distinctions in the work environment. (NOTE: for ease in reading this chapter, the term "college" is used to describe post-secondary institutions in general.)

The Students

College students are usually high school graduates, so they range in age from the late teen years to older adult learners in senior citizens programs. Increasing numbers of adults in their 30s and 40s are returning for a college degree. Men and women are equally represented in most institutions. Students are diverse and campus communities include racial and ethnic minority students, international students, and disabled students. Although most students attend full time, increasing numbers of students enroll part time, taking longer to complete their degree because of the need to work for financial support or meet family obligations. Most college students are highly motivated and have freely chosen to attend. They often want help with their personal growth and with ensuring their college success. On some campuses, staff may also help faculty, college alumni, and local community members.

Why Work in Postsecondary Education?

Rewards abound in working with all kinds of college students. The traditional college student is in an exciting transition from the family environment to the independence of becoming an adult. Older college students are enjoying the learning they might not have been able to pursue at a younger age. They are often making a career change or seeking professional advancement and see further education as essential to that goal. Except for the occasional student who feels pressured to go to college and might not want to be there, most students want to succeed and readily work with helping professionals and faculty to learn and grow.

Whatever the type of college, postsecondary institutions are exciting work environments. Day-to-day life might include concerts and plays, controversial speakers, breakthrough scientific discoveries, athletic events, and international food festivals. Staff and faculty colleagues are highly educated and function as professionals with autonomy, yet usually enjoy working together to solve problems in committees and task forces.

Staff in these settings are salaried employees with benefits such as health plans, paid vacation, and retirement programs. An additional benefit at some schools is allowing the staff member and dependents some tuition-free credits at that institution. So, working in college settings means:

- motivated students who respond to help;
- meaningful work that makes a difference in students' lives;
- exciting work environments;
- highly educated colleagues; and
- good benefits.

Preparing for Student Affairs Positions

Educational Qualifications

Most positions in student affairs require counseling and human development graduate degrees. Student affairs functions also include some specialties that require their own professional credentials; for example, the college health service would hire physicians and nurses; campus safety and security would hire law enforcement specialists; the chaplain would be an ordained clergy member; and food services would hire dietitians, nutritionists, and hotel and restaurant administration professionals.

Most entry level or beginning student affairs positions require at least a master's degree [Master of Arts (MA), Master of Science (MS), or Master of Education (MEd)] in one of several majors: guidance and counseling, college counseling, college student personnel, or higher education administration. Common doctoral degrees [Doctor of Education (EdD) or Doctor of Philosophy (PhD)]include college counseling, counselor education, counseling psychology, college student personnel administration, or higher education administration. Although undergraduate degrees in psychology or other behavioral sciences are desirable for some majors such as counseling, most college student personnel and higher education administration programs will consider many different undergraduate majors. Depending on the particular graduate program, graduate study includes such courses as counseling theory, counseling assessment, developmental theories of late adolescence and adulthood, career and group counseling, courses on understanding the college environment, administrative and management issues, history of higher education, or higher education law. Some positions will require a specialist degree whereas others prefer a broad, generalist background.

Begin Preparing as a College Student

Undergraduate college students can explore their interest in student affairs positions in many ways. There are several paid paraprofessional positions that provide intensive training and close professional supervision such as (a) resident assistants who live in a residence hall and plan programs, develop community, handle discipline, and advise residents; (b) peer advisors who work in special programs in the counseling center, academic advising center, minority centers, or career center to handle special programs and work individually with other students, performing academic tutoring and learning assistance; as well as (c) student employees who work in student affairs offices. Many students get volunteer experiences on and off campus as (a) elected student leaders in student government, clubs, organizations, church groups, community service, sports, student union programming, and campus media; (b) selected leaders for positions such as orientation advisors, first-year student mentors, hot-line workers, minority advisors, or members of student advisory boards for various offices; or (c) members of organizations and attendees at various campus functions. On some campuses students can sign up for specialty education like leadership retreats or women's awareness symposia, or enroll for credit in leadership, health education, or peer advising courses.

Student Affairs Functions

Most colleges are organized into three major units: (a) the curriculum (the academic program), (b) the co-curriculum (support services for students and experiences that aid their development outside of the classroom and success inside the classroom), and (c) the various business and administrative functions of the college. Student affairs functions encompass the entire co-curriculum and generally include the following functions, programs, and offices:

- Academic advising
- Admissions
- Athletics (intercollegiate, intramural sports, and recreation)
- Career planning and placement
- Chaplain and religious services
- Child care center
- Commuter student services and programs

- Counseling center
- Disabled student services
- Discipline and judicial programs
- Experiental learning (including cooperative education)
- Financial aid
- Food service
- Greek group advising (sororities and fraternities)
- Health service
- International student programs and study abroad
- Leadership development
- Learning skills and academic support services
- Minority student services (for example, Black student union; Hispanic center; women's center; or gay, lesbian, and/or bisexual program)
- National or regional testing centers
- Orientation and entry services
- Placement
- Reentry program (e.g., returning adult programs, adult education, continuing education)
- Registration and records
- Research, assessment, and evaluation office
- Residence life and housing (including summer conferences)
- Retention and enrollment management
- Safety and security
- Student activities
- Student employment
- Student media advising (campus newspaper, yearbook, radio, or TV station)
- Student union/student center
- Veterans' affairs
- Volunteer services

On some campuses, several of these functions might not be student affairs responsibilities; for example, in small colleges, faculty also do academic advising, or financial aid may report through business affairs. On some small campuses, one office might handle many functions such as orientation, student activities, and leadership development, whereas in large universities, one function like orientation may have several full-time staff. Some functions may not exist at all in some institutions. For example, most community colleges have no residence hall program. On some large campuses, academic advising and other student support services may be located within academic units like colleges and prefer that advisors have academic majors from that college.

Student Affairs Careers

Counseling and human development professionals work in many different areas. Student affairs functions that require other specialties (for example, health services, campus safety, or religious life) are not reviewed in this section. For each of the functional areas the following information is included: (a) examples of responsibilities, (b) nature of work with students, (c) qualifications, and (d) common job titles.

Academic Support Services and Academic Advising

Responsibilities. Academic support services include academic advising, learning skills centers, academic tutoring services, writing laboratories, and special clinics. In academic advising centers, staff work with individual students to plan academic schedules to meet college requirements. These staff are aware of support services and refer students to the counseling center or career development center as needed. Learning skill centers conduct individual and group sessions on such topics as time management, study skills, learning styles, and effective note taking. They often coordinate various academic subject tutoring programs. Special programs may exist for student athletes, minority students, students returning to college after many years (often called reentry services), highly able students completing several majors concurrently, those for whom English is a second language, and underprepared students. Such programs exist at all types of colleges and are larger in colleges where students need more help. *Nature of work with students*: These specialists work intensively with students in one-to-one relationships and small group work over extended periods of time. Some students may be required to attend as a condition of their provisional enrollment, but most voluntarily seek services to improve their academic skills. *Qualifications*: Staff in these programs are usually counselors with a master's degree and special training in learning differences and learning skills. *Common job titles*: Director or Assistant Director of Academic Advising, Academic Advisor, Director or Assistant Director of Learning Skills Center, Coordinator of Special Services, Learning Skills Specialist.

Administration and Leadership of Student Affairs

Responsibilities. The chief student affairs officer (CSAO) is the supervisor of all student affairs departments and functions, often working with or through other department heads and interacting with faculty, parents, alumni, and community members. This person is responsible for staffing, budgeting, planning, implementing policy and procedures, and representing student interests with academic and business affairs administrators. This person commonly serves on the cabinet of the president of the college and, in some institutions, may report to a provost or executive vice president. *Nature of work with students*: The chief student affairs officer works with student advisors and student leaders, mediates in student conflict, and is involved with crisis situations. On larger campuses, CSAOs work primarily with staff, and on smaller campuses, they may provide direct services to students. *Qualifications*: This is a senior-level position requiring extensive job experience and usually a doctoral degree. A graduate degree in college student personnel/development or higher education administration is preferred. *Common job titles include*: Vice President, Vice-Chancellor, or Dean of Student Affairs/Student Development (average salary: $50,256).

A special comment on salaries. Salary ranges have not been included due to the tremendous diversity in pay between types of institutions and level of position. Each fall, a complete comparative salary review is published in *The Chronicle of Higher Education* (a weekly newspaper in higher education available in most college libraries or administrative offices). Generally, staff with doctorates earn more than those with master's degrees; higher level positions like deans or vice presidents are paid more than entry staff positions. Depending on the type of campus and previous experience, vice presidents or deans may earn $30,000 to $80,000; directors of major programs earn from $30,000 to $50,000; staff in entry-level positions earn from the high teens to mid-$20s. The 1988–1989 actual average salary for all types of institutions is included where available, but refers generally to upper-management positions. (Source: *The Chronicle of Higher Education*, September 6, 1989, p. 20.)

Admissions, Registration, and Enrollment Management

Responsibilities. This unit often performs two separate functions and may report either to student affairs or academic affairs. On small college campuses, admissions sometimes reports directly to the president. Admissions involves identifying, attracting, and admitting students qualified to enroll at the college. This function includes recruitment; screening; conducting interviews; evaluating academic transcripts; visiting secondary school guidance officers; participating in college night fairs; designing publications such as videos, catalogs, and view books; and communicating with large numbers of applicants. Special functions include enrollment management. This includes programs to retain enrolled students and recruiting special populations such as Black students. Beginning jobs usually require travel to recruit and may involve regional, national, and international travel. Once students are admitted, the registrar's office maintains and monitors their academic progress. The function includes publishing course schedules, registering students for courses, handling changes in schedules once classes are under way, issuing official transcripts of credits and diplomas earned, and maintaining statistical data. *Nature of work with students*: Admissions staff have many short-term contacts with prospective students and parents and help them match their needs and interests with the right institution, which may not even be the institution of employment for the admissions officer. Registrars work with most students through their records and occasionally see students in person to process their schedules and provide services. *Qualifications*: Director-level jobs require experience and a master's or doctoral degree in college student personnel or higher education administration. Admissions officers on some campuses are bachelor's degree staff, often graduates of that institution, or may have master's degrees in counseling fields or college student personnel. Some positions require marketing experience as well. Registrars have a variety of degrees but must demonstrate administrative and management skills and computer literacy. Beginning staff often travel, and remuneration includes a travel allowance or use of a college car.

Common job titles: Assistant, Associate and/or Director or Dean of Admissions or Admissions and Records, Registrar, Director of Enrollment Management, Coordinator of School Relations, Transfer Admissions Specialist, Admissions Officer or Admissions Counselor (average Admissions Director salary: $39,500; Registrar: $35,400; Enrollment Management Director, $44,168).

Athletics (Intercollegiate, Intramural, and Recreation Programs)

Responsibilities: Intercollegiate athletics include those men's and women's major and minor sports teams that play other colleges. Athletic directors maintain standards, schedule sport facilities, recruit, train and coach individual sports, and ensure academic progress of student athletes. On some campuses coaches might also teach physical education courses. Intramural programs often report through athletics although they can be organized separately. They include club sports, campus competitions between student organizations such as fraternities and sororities, residence halls, and faculty and staff leagues. Recreation programs include intramural programs and free play, outing clubs, tournaments, and games. The director of intercollegiate athletics often reports to the chief student affairs officer or to the college president. *Nature of work with students*: Athletics staff have extensive individual and group contact with students around common sports interests. Those who work with intercollegiate athletes are involved with many aspects of student athletes' lives. Those in athletic academic support units work individually with students on learning skills, tutoring, study skills, and personal issues. *Qualifications*: Many of these positions require physical education or recreation degrees or direct athletic experience; the academic support services require counseling, counseling psychology, and college student development specialists who can work individually with athletes. On some small campuses, recreation and intramural programs may be part of student activities. *Common job titles*: Director of Intercollegiate Athletics, Intramurals, or Recreation, Coach, Athletic Academic Support Advisor, Athletic Academic Advisor, or Recreation Aide. (Average salaries: Director of Athletics, $44,350; Director of Men's Athletics, $42,034; Director of Women's Athletics, $32,600; Director, Campus Recreation and Intramurals, $29,150.)

Career Development and Placement

Responsibilities: This department usually reports to the chief student affairs officer but is occasionally found within an academic college. Career development functions include counseling about career choice or choice of major, individual assessment, occupational testing, maintaining an occupational resource library, coordinating alumni and community mentor programs, serving as liaison with academic departments, and providing life planning programs. Placement responsibilities include solicitation of prospective employers, developing job referral networks, maintaining credential files, assisting with job development services and job interviewing skills, and providing transition to work. Placement functions often include summer employment, part-time local work, and, coordination of internships and cooperative education. *Nature of work with students*: Placement includes individual and group work with students. Staff may teach credit courses focusing on expanding the student's knowledge of the world of work. Career development professionals frequently work with first-year students and sophomores engaged in life planning. Placement professionals work with juniors and seniors. Work involves counseling, teaching, and advising. Students may come to talk about career issues but also have other issues to resolve such as indecision and uncertainty, so frequent referral is made to the mental health or vocational counselors or psychologists. *Qualifications*: Positions require a master's degree in counseling, college student personnel/development, or higher education with emphasis on student development. Directors usually need a doctoral degree and extensive career experience. *Common job titles*: Assistant, Associate, or Director of Career Planning and Placement, Director of Career Development Center, Career Counselor, Career Consultant (average salary: Director of Placement, $32,404).

Commuter Programs and Off-Campus Housing

Responsibilities: Commuter students may be those who come from the region near campus and live at home with their parents, in their own homes, in apartments, or have moved from elsewhere to live near campus. On many campuses, commuter students compose the majority of the student body. Staff who work in commuter programs and off-campus housing programs serve as commuter advocates, provide off-campus housing and roommate locator services, help with commuter parking, or provide shuttle bus services. They keep other campus offices aware of commuter student needs. *Nature of work with students*: Commuter student staff provide direct services to commuters and may work with commuter student advisors. *Qualifications*: These offices frequently seek master's degree staff with college student personnel or higher education administration degrees and strong administration, management, and programming skills. Candidates must be aware of adult student issues. *Common job titles*: Director or Assistant Director of Commuter Programs, Commuter Student Advisor, or Coordinator of Off-Campus Housing.

Counseling and Testing

Responsibilities: Counseling and testing services are usually located in a counseling service with a director and a staff of psychologists or counselors. Staff work with individuals and groups on such issues as academic success, relationships, test anxiety, sexual concerns, career development, depression, self-esteem, suicide, substance abuse, or eating disorders. Services are usually remedial, developmental, and preventive. Staff provide outreach programming to students in other settings such as residence halls or student organizations and are frequently consultants to faculty and other professional staff (see chapter 5). Counselors aid students and other staff with crisis situations. Counselors may teach courses in human relations skills or learning and communications skills. Testing is employed to support the assessment process in counseling or to help students who need standardized tests (for example, the Graduate Record Examination, GED, etc.). Counseling services usually engage in some research to help understand student development and the counseling process. *Nature of work with students*: Counselors work confidentially with individual students and small groups of students to explore student issues of concern. Students may seek assistance with normal developmental life issues or more complex forms of personality dysfunction. The director performs administrative and management functions and, on smaller campuses, may also counsel individual students. Counselors occasionally refer students to psychiatrists in the campus health services or in off-campus agencies. *Qualifications*: Staff commonly need a doctoral degree in guidance and counseling, counseling, counseling psychology, or clinical psychology. On larger campuses, they may be affiliated with the graduate teaching program in counseling, psychology, or college student development. In many cases they need to qualify for licensure in the state in which the college is located. Smaller colleges or community colleges may hire staff with master's degrees for the same functions. *Common job titles*: Director of Counseling, Staff Counselor, Staff Psychologist, Counselor, Counseling Psychologist, Clinical Psychologist, Training Director, or Psychometrist (a specialist in testing). (Average salary of the Director is $38,100.)

Disabled Student Services

Responsibilities: This office provides direct assistance to students with various disabilities. Staff work with other campus offices to ensure an effective campus environment for the disabled student. Staff coordinate such programs as interpreter and note taking services for the hearing impaired, accessibility maps and advocacy for the physically challenged, computer services, and special testing programs for learning disabled students. Staff coordinate residence hall accommodations for those with hearing, sight, and mobility challenges; special parking and transportation systems; academic support; and generally serve in an advocacy role, helping the campus adapt to needs of special students. Staff work closely with state vocational rehabilitation services. *Nature of work with students*: Staff work individually with students to assess needs and maintain supports. *Qualifications*: Staff usually need a master's degree and benefit from study in rehabilitation counseling. *Common job titles*: Director or Assistant Director of Disabled Student Services, Counselor, Learning Disability Specialist, or Interpreter.

Discipline and Judicial Programs

Responsibilities: These functions are often part of other roles such as the dean or assistant dean of students, director of residence life or, on large campuses, there may be separate offices of judicial affairs. These staff meet with individual students accused of violations of campus policies such as cheating (called academic dishonesty), alcohol or drug violations, vandalism, fighting, and infractions of law or other community standards. Violations may be handled by the judicial affairs officer or a student judicial board. Staff gather information needed to understand each case, train board members, ensure fairness and due process, maintain judicial records, help individual violators understand the nature of their problems, and engage in moral and ethical reasoning. *Nature of work with students*: Judicial officers work with student judicial board members, and hold individual sessions with students who need to understand complex regulations and the consequences of their actions. Staff often refer students for counseling to understand their behavior. *Qualifications*: Positions require a master's degree in college student personnel or higher education administration. Larger campuses may also require a law degree or legal coursework. *Common job titles*: Director of Judicial Programs, Judicial Program Advisor, Dean or Assistant Dean of Students.

Experiential Learning and Volunteerism

Responsibilities: Experiential learning and volunteerism offices may be either in student affairs or academic affairs. The experiential learning staff coordinate practical experiences for students outside the classroom. These fieldwork experiences include paid and unpaid internships, practica, cooperative education, and volunteer experiences. Such experiences may be for academic credit or for no credit. Cooperative education includes learning experiences closely related to an academic major. *Nature of work with students*: Staff work individually with many students to match their needs with a meaningful experience, work with supervisors on site, and manage student records. *Qualifications*: Staff usually have a master's degree in counseling, college student personnel, or higher education administration. They may also have experience in an academic discipline that had a cooperative education program. *Common job titles*: Director or Assistant Director of Experiential Learning or Cooperative Education, Director of Volunteer Programs.

Financial Aid and Student Employment

Responsibilities: Many students need financial assistance to enroll or remain enrolled in college. Financial aid officers counsel individual students and their families and assist them in receiving appropriate forms of aid. They work with such programs as college work study, campus employment, federal and state aid programs, loan programs, and private and public scholarships and grants. They advise students about personal economic matters, help with financial planning and budgeting, maintain eligibility records, review and award aid packages, and often coordinate job referral. The director usually reports to the chief student affairs officer but may report to the dean of admissions or vice president for business affairs. Student employment staff coordinate work placement, aid students in interviews, and maintain employment records. *Nature of work with students*: Financial aid officers have extensive contact with students in financial need and students in distress about their funds, and have extensive contact with students and families about forms, records, and employment. *Qualifications*: Financial aid administration is a complex speciality with many regulations and procedures. A master's in higher education administration or college student personnel is a common entry requirement, but employers also prefer computer literacy and financial aid experience. This job requires knowledge of employment regulations. *Common job titles*: Director, Dean, or Assistant in Financial Aid, Student Support, or Campus Employment, Student Employment Coordinator. (Average salary for the Director is $34,032.)

Minority Student Services

Responsibilities: Various multicultural, gender, ethnic, or racial groups benefit from special services designed to form community and meet special needs. Such programs include Black or African-American student organizations; Asian student groups; Native American student groups; Hispanic centers; or international student offices. Other programs might include women's centers; or gay, lesbian, and/or bisexual student organizations. Staff working with these programs advise students individually, plan topical programs, serve as advocates for these students on campus, educate campus staff and faculty about special needs, and provide support programs. Small colleges may not have separate centers. *Nature of work with students*: Staff interact socially and academically with individual students and groups of students. The office or center may become a home base, and students drop by regularly, providing both informal and formal contact. *Qualifications*: Staff must have a master's degree in counseling or college student personnel, or from another major such as Black studies, women's studies, or international education. On some campuses, staff may hold a joint appointment with an academic department. Frequently staff are members of the special group with whom they are working (for example, a women's center usually has women staff). *Common job titles*: Director or Assistant Director of the Center, Black Student Advisor, Director of Minority Programs, International Student Advisor. (Average salary: Director of Minority Affairs, $33,800; Director of International Students, $31,400.)

Orientation and Entry Services

Responsibilities: Staff in these offices aid new students in their adjustment to campus life. They work primarily with first-year students and transfer students at the time they first enroll. They design and coordinate orientation sessions for new students, including placement testing to determine appropriate course levels; provide discussions of campus life and course advising; teach orientation courses; design orientation mailings; conduct parent and family programs; and host parents' or family weekends. *Nature of work with students*: Orientation staff supervise upper-class orientation leaders and work individually and in groups with new students. *Qualifications*: Master's degrees in counseling, college student personnel, or higher education administration are required with work experience in new student issues. *Common job titles include*: Director or Assistant Director of Orientation, Dean of Freshmen, Coordinator of Freshman Experience.

Residence Life and Housing

Responsibilities: Residence life staff are specialists in group living, peer interaction, and community building. Staff are concerned with educational and social programming, roommate compatibility, floor standards, discipline, crisis management, and individual and group development. Entry-level staff supervise undergraduate student staff (often called resident assistants or RAs), and building custodial and security staff. Residence halls may be single-sex, coeducational, living-learning centers, or special interest housing such as athletic halls, married student housing, graduate housing, apartment housing, fraternity/sorority, international student housing, off-campus housing for commuters, or faculty housing. These offices often manage a summer conference program to use residence facilities on a year-round basis. Hall sizes range from 50 to over 1,000 residents per building. Entry staff personnel usually live in their residence hall. Residence life programs are usually the largest employer of student affairs professionals. *Nature of work with students*: Entry staff work intensely with students in a live-in, 24-hour-per-day situation. They interact with students in multiple settings and around complex needs such as adjustment to college, discipline, programming, and personal advising. Assistant directors might work with staff selection, training, and development. *Qualifications*: Most positions require a master's degree in counseling, college student personnel, or higher education administration. Some campuses have graduate students living in residence and hire professionals with a master's degree as the area directors who supervise a number of graduate assistants. When positions are live-in, remuneration usually includes a salary plus apartment and utilities. *Common job titles*: Director of Housing and Residence Life, Area Coordinator, Commuity Director, Hall Director, Head Resident, Training Director, Area Manager, Facilities Director, and Business Manager. (Average Director of Student Housing salary, $30,625.)

Student Activities

Responsibilities: Staff usually advise student organizations; coordinate leadership development programs; schedule nonacademic campus space; advise student government organizations; work with student media such as radio or newspapers; publish the student handbook or yearbook; develop, enforce, and interpret rules and regulations; and develop and implement a broad range of campus cultural, social, and educational programming. This office is challenged to meet the diverse interests of many campus groups. *Nature of work with students*: Activities staff work closely with individual student leaders and with students in groups/organizations. Work is fast paced, with many students regularly in and out of a busy office. *Qualifications*: These positions require a master's degree in college student personnel or higher education administration, competence in student development theory, and skills such as consulting, program planning, and advising. In addition, these positions may require experience in the entertainment or fine arts areas. Counseling degrees are also acceptable with administrative skill and experience. *Common job titles*: Dean, Director, Associate or Assistant Dean of Student Activities, Director of Campus Activities, Student Activity Advisor or Counselor, Director of Greek Life, or Panhellenic or Intrafraternity Council Advisor (Average salary: Director of Student Activities, $28,530).

Student Union Programming and Student Union Administration

Responsibilities: The student union is the "living room" of the campus: usually a centrally located building with many services such as the bookstore, lounges, meeting rooms, movie theater, bowling lanes, ballroom, cafeterias and restaurants, branch bank, student government offices, and student affairs offices. Professional staff schedule space; raise money; plan programs such as film festivals, cultural festivals, recreation and tournaments, or topical forums; and advise student programming boards. *Nature of work with students*: This job involves close work with student leaders such as student union programming boards and frequent contact with a broad cross-section of students. Some large student unions have over 20,000 student visits per day. *Qualifications*: Most student union staff need a master's degree in college student personnel or higher education administration with strong administration, management, and programming skills. *Common job titles*: Director, Assistant or Associate Director of the Student Union or Campus Union, Programming Coordinator or Advisor. (Average salary: Director of Student Union, $36,936).

Involvement and Support

When you take a position in student affairs, there are many professional associations and opportunities for involvement. In addition to the American Association for Counseling and Development (AACD), numerous general professional societies such as the American College Personnel Association (ACPA), the National Association of Student Personnel Administrators (NASPA), or the National Association of Women Deans, Administrators and Counselors (NAWDAC) and speciality associations such as the American College and University Housing Officers International (ACUHOI), the National Association of Campus Activities (NACA), or the National Orientation Directors Association (NODA) provide special journals, ethical standards, professional development activities, and leadership opportunities. Professionals have many opportunities to meet on campus, in the region, or at national or international conventions. Staff expect each other to share new programs, research findings, and improved approaches to common problems. When faced with a perplexing problem at work, staff just pick up the telephone and call professional colleagues who are always ready to help. Student affairs professionals work in a collaborative, sharing, and supportive field.

For more information on careers in student affairs work requiring counseling and human development credentials, talk with a student affairs professional at a college near you. Attend a program sponsored at a nearby college during "National Careers in Student Affairs Week" (usually the last week in October), attend a conference in the state or region (see listings in the *Chronicle of Higher Education*), or read the following publications in "Recommended Readings."

Recommended Readings

American College Personnel Association. (1979). *Consider the college student development profession*. Commission XII: Graduate Preparation Programs. Alexandria, VA: American College Personnel Association. (A pamphlet overviewing work in student affairs.)

CAS standards and guidelines for student services/development programs. C/O Vice President for Student Affairs, the University of Maryland, College Park, 20742. (Contains standards for graduate preparation programs and for most student affairs functional areas.)

Delworth, U., Hansen, G. R., & Assoc. (1989). *Student services: A handbook for the profession* (2nd ed.). San Francisco: Jossey-Bass. (A textbook used in many first-year master's degree programs.)

Kiem, M.B., & Graham, J. (Eds). (1987). *A directory of graduate preparation programs in college student personnel*. A publication of the American College

Personnel Association—Commission XII: Graduate Preparation Programs. Carbondale, IL: Southern Illinois University. (Contains graduate entrance requirements, master's and doctoral curriculum, and information about graduate faculty of over 100 graduate programs.)

Kirby, A.F., & Woodard, D. (Eds). (1983). *Career perspectives in student affairs*. NASPA Monograph Series, Vol. 1. Washington, DC: National Association of Student Personnel Administrators. (Contains chapters for new professionals, women, and career advancement issues.)

Rentz, A.L., & Saddlemire, G.L. (Eds). (1988). *Student affairs functions in higher education*. Springfield, IL: Charles C Thomas. (Describes the work in many functional areas and career paths in student affairs.)

Associations for Further Information (See appendix for addresses)

American College Personnel Association
Association of College and University Housing Officers International
National Association for Campus Activities
National Association for Women Deans, Administrators, & Counselors
National Association of Student Personnel Administrators
National Orientation Directors Association

Chapter 5

CONSULTING CAREERS IN COLLEGE SETTINGS

Clyde A. Crego

The many roles of counselors and psychologists who provide comprehensive services to college campuses include a relatively new, specialized function, that of campus-based consultant. This role has evolved over the past 40 years as campus mental health and human development specialists have needed to reach larger numbers of student "clients" than can be seen on a one-to-one counseling basis. This need resulted in the development of a consultation component within campus counseling services.

Why Campus-Based Consultation?

Did you ever think that you might like to make conditions better for several hundred, or even several thousand, people and yet never talk with any of them on a face-to-face basis? If your answer is "Yes," then consultation might be a good career to consider. *Consultation* is a process by which human service experts provide specialized, time-limited assistance to organizations. Types of consultation vary from highly focused problem-solving assistance to more global services that can be applied to a wide range of organizational situations. Expertise in consultation is acquired in academic training programs or postgraduate work.

There are three reasons why campus mental health professionals conduct campus consultations: prevention, economics, and education. Prevention programs often utilize the consultation skills of counseling professionals for the initial definition and development of specific prevention programs. Experts might consult with student services personnel to design and develop programs that can reach more students and help them function

49

more effectively. This is economically attractive to administrators concerned about organizational efficiency and program relevance. Consultation based on the education/training of other professionals often focuses
on helping faculty, staff, and administrators solve their own problems, or
on the development of new skills such as improved interpersonal communication.

Prevention

Student development theory, research, and experience with college
students who acquire problem-solving skills via counseling, have all created an intense interest in the concept of prevention. Mental health professionals in general society have also become interested in prevention to
help people develop their personal growth and general life skills, and
reduce the negative effects of stressful events or experiences that may
block growth or learning. Campus counseling staffs have developed prevention programs for college students, who benefit from special programs
with a strong prevention focus. Consultation or training to develop a
prevention focus with campus faculty and staff who work directly with
students represents "indirect" services that can have a wide impact on
campus. For instance, improving campus environments to reduce stress
on students represents one type of campus consultation and program development (Banning & Kaiser, 1974). Multidisciplinary consultation teams,
including campus counselors and psychologists, can make campus environments more responsive to the needs of individual students.

Economics

Campus budgets have been cut in the past several decades concurrently with increased demand for student services. This has caused campus-
based counselors and psychologists to develop new kinds of services or
roles that "spread" their skills and knowledge about student development,
problem prevention, and problem remediation across a wider number of
students than can be seen on an individual basis. Consultants can reach
more students by working through other campus professionals than if they
worked with students on a one-to-one basis. This may include the training
of staff who have primary contact with students, such as academic advisors
or campus police. This improves the chance for early remediation of
student problems. For example, campus police frequently encounter students in the beginning stages of personal crises, and are in a unique role
to help those students assess their situations and to seek appropriate mea-
sures to block further development of nonadaptive behaviors.

Education

A goal in education is to have all campus personnel respond appropriately to troubled students they encounter. Campus police, residence hall personnel, faculty, administrators, and others all can profit from organizational training in psychological skill development, management techniques, and conflict resolution techniques. These have long been accepted by corporations, government agencies, and social service agencies as needed skills. Colleges and universities are also recognizing the need for staff to have specific skill training.

Counselors and counseling psychologists often function as the campus-based consultants who train college staffs in techniques designed to improve organizational efficiency, respond to human needs or individual differences, function in crisis situations, or enhance student and employee morale.

Consulting with campus units to design student development programs for specific groups of students represents an additional activity in which counseling staffs may "export" their knowledge and skills by training other persons to work with students. Peer counseling programs use this approach, often with a campus consultant to assist them.

Some counseling staffs in educational institutions spend as much as 50% of their time engaged in this kind of campus-based consultation. This is an increasingly popular and viable role for counseling staff members.

Types of Campus-Based Consultation

Counselors and psychologists conduct several types of consultation that may include overlapping functions or highly specialized roles for the campus consultant. General types of consultation, along with an example of each, are described below.

Resource Consultation

Consulting with other campus units that are developing specific programs for students, as well as consulting about staff development, involves providing specialized resources such as information about specialty areas like cross-cultural counseling. Consultation may also involve conducting training to develop skills in personnel who work closely with students. Campus consultants utilize a variety of resources after an initial assessment of need. For instance, assisting clerical personnel at registration windows to improve communication with students may involve provision of self-training materials after determining what is needed, or may instead involve actually conducting the training. Linking the consumer (registration department and staff) to what is needed is the goal of this type of consultation.

Conflict Management Consultation

Sometimes campus groups of professionals, such as faculty administrators, are unable to resolve group-related problems without outside assistance. A consultant trained in special techniques for helping groups resolve conflicts may be able to help. Psychologically trained personnel are often experts in the areas of conflict resolution. A consultation model frequently used in this type of work is that employed by Schein (1969), called *process consultation*. Intergroup relations and group problem solving is the focus.

Training/Consultation

Campus groups or units often have a staff development need that can best be determined by a consultant who assesses which type of intervention might be most helpful in a specific situation. This assessment frequently results in the design of a training program to meet the established need. The training may be conducted by the consulting staff or by other training consultants. For example, campus student services workers wishing to improve their cross-cultural skills in working with highly diverse students often ask cross-cultural psychologists to help determine what would help develop cross-cultural sensitivity or provide a suitable cross-cultural program.

Crisis Intervention Consultation

This type of consultation can vary from working with campus personnel and students concerned about a student in crisis to consulting with organized campus units (and staff) about handling current concerns in the crisis area such as an increase in residence hall student suicide attempts, or excessive alcohol consumption at college-sponsored events. Frequently this form of consultation service occurs as a result of campus crisis experts' having established a formal system for assessing crises, intervening with specific students, and providing these consultative and referral services for other campus staff and faculty who encounter students in distress. Many forms of crisis intervention on the college campus adhere to the historically important work of Caplan (1970), who developed widely accepted principles of mental health consultation.

Campus Ecology Consultation

There is a small but growing number of campus-based counseling personnel who consult with campus administrators about how to redesign, construct, or modify institutionalized campus functions and external characteristics to improve their "fit" with the individual needs of diverse students. Campus ecology theorists agree that much of the stress that students experience on campus is environmentally induced rather than resulting from a so-called poor adjustment of individuals to a stress-inducing environment. These theorists sometimes criticize traditional forms of one-to-one counseling as attempts to adjust healthy individuals to unhealthy environments, resulting in stress or dysfunction. These workers most often utilize a formal type of organizational consultation to assist campuses in determining changeable sources of student stress caused by dysfunctional or inappropriately negative external (outside the person) factors. An example of a poor person-environment "fit" would be requiring all students who need to change class registrations (after classes have begun) to do so between the hours of 8:00 a.m. and 10:00 a.m. on a campus where 95% of all students have classes at those hours. Failure to change the registration hours (environment) to improve student access requires students to adjust to a poor environmental characteristic, resulting in unnecessary student stress. Often such rigid environments have many similar stressors. Formal consultation programs may help reduce, eliminate, or modify some of these stressors if the consultation is based on an understanding of how to introduce and manage change within organizations. Several theorists present models for changing campus environments that assist students to have needed developmental experiences (Huebner, 1979; Oetting, 1967; Morrill & Hurst, 1971).

Cross-Cultural Program Consultation

A specific approach used for making the environment more suitable for increasingly diverse student groups includes the work of cross-cultural counseling specialists. They work consultatively with the campus at-large to extend their knowledge and skill to campus personnel who interact with ethnic minority students. Counselors are frequently knowledgeable about cross-cultural information and interactive methods to improve campus environments to meet the needs of diverse minority groups. For example, some minority groups seriously underutilize services, including student services, that are often designed primarily for White, middle-class students (Padilla, Ruiz, & Alvarez, 1975). Consultation assistance to campus personnel based on cross-cultural counseling and research expertise is being applied to campus priorities such as improving retention and graduation rates of minority students.

Specialized Technical Consultation

Counseling personnel are frequently trained in advanced technical areas such as testing, the development of measurement techniques, evaluation research strategies, and general research methods for assessing student development. These specialized skills are often sought out by other student services workers and campus administrators to develop or improve campus programs that evaluate and describe individual differences among students. Campus departments that attempt to design programs based on assessed needs often turn to the consulting psychologist for help in designing and conducting needs assessments to help ensure that programs offered meet the needs of highly diverse student abilities, values, and interests.

Preparing to Be a Campus-Based Consultant

Graduate education that prepares college graduates for working as counselors or campus psychologists provides extensive training for working with students individually or in a group counseling context. Although much of the skill and knowledge gained in graduate programs "transfers" to the consulting arena, until recently few graduate programs provided specialized training in consulting itself. Success by campus-based consultants in creating this specialty among campus counseling staffs has helped stimulate a significant change in the number of courses offered in the area of consultation. This has been especially characteristic of the field of counseling psychology, whose graduates have had a great impact in creating psychological programs in counseling and human services on college campuses. The field of school psychology has also influenced the development of consultation programs for schools serving grades K through 12. The field of community psychology, often a branch of clinical psychology, has contributed rich theory and principles of application to the design of campus prevention programs.

Almost all of the training programs that now offer specific training in campus-based consultation require earning a doctoral degree (EdD, PsyD, or PhD) in counseling or counseling psychology. Graduate doctoral programs that are accredited by the American Psychological Association (APA) and the Council for Accreditation of Counseling and Related Educational Programs (CACREP) [see chapter 13] are the most likely to provide both coursework and practical experience in campus-based consultation, especially if the required internship at the end of the degree work is in an accredited counseling center. Choosing a graduate program that offers consultation training and emphasizes internships with a strong experiential training in consultation is the best route to become a campus-based consultant.

Many counseling center staffs include clinical psychologists who may have learned consultation techniques in their graduate training or work experience, especially if their programs emphasized community psychology. Although clinical psychology does not focus exclusively on working in educational settings, the skills training and core psychological education are nearly identical with those of counseling psychology. Clinical programs with a strong emphasis in health psychology, a subspecialty like community psychology, are also likely to include a consulting emphasis.

Specialists in consulting work applied to systems or organizations, such as the college or university campus, emphasize the importance of consultants-in-training preparing themselves by choosing to take courses at the graduate level in organizational psychology and advanced social psychology (Crego, 1985). Campus units or other types of organizations have their own characteristics and relationship to principles of change that go well beyond what is understood about how to change individuals (Levinson, 1972). Learning as much as possible about the nature of organizations will enhance the work of the consultant in any setting, especially of those working in organizational settings.

Characteristics of Consulting Psychologists

Consulting psychologists must have an intense interest in psychology in general, applied psychology and counseling in particular, and have the intellectual ability to succeed in competitive graduate education. In addition, consulting specialists develop a strong attraction to working with organizations in ways that require them to assess organizational characteristics and determine how change can be made so that persons can function effectively. Ability and interest in utilizing skills beyond those involved in relationship counseling—such as being assertive with leaders, taking on a diagnostic role when assessing organizational characteristics involved in doing a consultation, and ability to shift roles easily—all imply a role capacity and complexity not always seen among traditional human services workers. Flexibility, strong evaluation skills, and the ability to develop strong creative skills for performing unique consultation assignments all lead to becoming a successful consultant. After training in applied psychology, a person is required to learn in a self-directed way by seeking experience in consultation activity with consultants, and through reading in areas such as organizational development and social psychology.

Finding a Graduate Program

With undergraduate degree work, the aim is to achieve a broad education in psychological and human relations theory, research, and elementary applied psychology. The serious student should begin to seek information about graduate programs early in the junior year. Doctoral programs that have developed a strong component in the subspecialty of consulting through coursework and by providing experiential training should be explored at this time. Undergraduate professors may be helpful in sharing their knowledge about various elements and specializations within the major fields of psychology and counseling. Students may also write to the American Psychological Association (APA) for their reference book that describes all of the major graduate programs in psychology. Students may also write to the secretaries of the APA Division of Consulting Psychology, the Division of Community Psychology, and the Division of Counseling Psychology about programs that best prepare graduate students in campus-based and general consultation. The Council for Accreditation of Counseling and Related Educational Programs (CACREP) also can provide information on accreditation of graduate programs in counseling (see chapter 13).

Undergraduate college students also may wish to visit their campus counseling or career centers to determine whether staff members in those student services can provide information about preparation in the professional areas leading to becoming a campus-based consultant.

On some campuses, ongoing human services projects use paid or volunteer students who wish to gain experience. This is especially characteristic of campuses with extensive programs in paraprofessional counseling that provide human relations skills training to volunteers. Student development staff members who operate paraprofessional programs utilizing students as helpers are often interested and involved in campus-based consultation activity.

The Future of Campus-Based Consultants

As the college campus becomes more complex, and as the student body becomes more diverse, it will become increasingly difficult to serve the majority of student with programs designed to meet the needs of an exclusive group of students. Reaching greater numbers of students through working with campus systems and personnel will gain attention in student services. There will be increased emphasis on outreach counseling and indirect services to extend psychological expertise across as wide a range of student development issues and students as possible. The campus professionals who can function in campus subenvironments outside the walls of their home departments need courage, creativity, and persistence to apply their skills within organizations that seem to create stress or failure for some of their members. The opportunity to alleviate student stress by working with other campus professionals on a consultative basis and to facilitate organizational relevance to wider numbers of student learners has never been greater.

Consulting to Off-Campus Institutions

Experienced campus-based consultants with skills in specialized ares of counseling may provide consultation services off-campus. Colleges and universities needing expert assistance in program development, program evaluation, program administration, or managing organizational conflict may seek outside consultation in areas such as training program development, student services, special programming, or program organization/administration.

Consultation provides a unique opportunity for student services units or administrations to assist students in a constructive way via program self-assessment procedures. Assistance may range from attempts to resolve conflict within or between campus units to proactive program construction accompanying new program development. Unique types of consultation have been developed, such as those required by schools seeking accreditation of programs or services.

Why Consult Off Campus?

Consultation performed by student services experts is consistent with higher education philosophy in general (shared knowledge across units within academic fields), and with professional goals that dictate that human services workers train and enable others to apply effective practice on behalf of students as learners or students as consumers of services.

Consultation to other organizations provides highly experienced and knowledgeable student services personnel with the opportunity to augment income as professional consultants. Many educator-consultants have fees that range from $500 to $1,200 a day plus expenses. Student services personnel are committed to benefiting from and contributing to professional associations with other educators and professionals. These experiences range from informal networks of colleagues to formal organized associations such as the American Association for Counseling and Development (AACD), its many divisions, such as the American College

Personnel Association (ACPA), or the Division of Counseling Psychology of the American Psychological Association. The ACPA is organized into commissions that provide an opportunity to form professional networks, including consultative networks. Innovative student services program developers frequently present their work at the annual meetings of these professional associations. Leadership in creative programming may also lead to consulting opportunities.

A specialized form of consultation is preparing specific student services units, or training programs associated with them, to become accredited. For instance, the International Association of Counseling Services (IACS), an affiliate of AACD, accredits campus counseling centers. Likewise, APA accredits doctoral degree and internship programs, many of which are associated with campus-based student services. The accrediting body frequently requires preaccreditation consultation from its list of highly experienced and skilled accreditation site visitors. This is a good example of a proactive, planned approach to using evaluation-consultation to improve services and counseling training programs.

Consultation helps advance the development of student services programs to meet the unique needs of students. Consultation helps to "institutionalize" student services programs, advance their credibility, and strengthen the staffs that operate them.

Further Information

Further information about these occupations can be obtained from your counselor or career center. Professional associations that can provide information are listed below; their addresses are found in the appendix.

Consultant: American Psychological Association (Division— Consulting Psychology); American College Personnel Association; National Association of Student Personnel Administrators.

Two books about consultation can give you additional information. They are the Gallessich (1982) and the Huebner and Corazzini (1984) references included in the Reference list that follows.

References

Banning, J.H., & Kaiser, L. (1974). An ecological perspective and model for campus design. *Personnel and Guidance Journal, 52,* 370–375.
Caplan, G. (1970). *The theory and practice of mental health consultation.* New York: Basic Books.

Crego, C.A. (1985). Ethics of consultation: The need for improved consultation training. *The Counseling Psychologist, 13,* 473–476.

Gallessich, J. (1982). *The profession and practice of consultation.* San Francisco: Jossey-Bass.

Huebner, L.A. (1979). Emergent issues of theory and practice. In L.A. Huebner (Ed.), *New directions for student services—Redesigning campus environments* (pp. 1–21). San Francisco: JosseyBass.

Huebner, L.A., & Corazzini, J.J. (1984). Environmental assessment and intervention. In S.C. Brown, & R.W. Lent (Eds.), *Handbook of counseling psychology* (pp. 579–621). New York: Wiley-Interscience.

Levinson, H. (Ed.). (1972). *Organizational diagnosis.* Cambridge, MA: Harvard University Press.

Morrill, W.H., & Hurst, J.C. (1971). A preventive and developmental role for the college counselor. *The Counseling Psychologist, 2*(4), 90–95.

Oetting, E.R. (1967). A developmental definition of counseling psychology. *Journal of Counseling Psychology, 14,* 382–385.

Padilla, A.M., Ruiz, R.A., & Alvarez, R. (1975). Community mental health services for the Spanish-speaking/surnamed population. *American Psychologist, 30,* 892–905.

Schein, E.H. (1969). *Process consultation: Its role in organizational development.* Reading, MA: Addison-Wesley.

Chapter 6

CAREERS IN BUSINESS AND INDUSTRY

Bree Hayes

When people imagine counselors or other helping professionals at work, they typically picture them in settings like schools, mental health centers, hospitals, or private practices. Also, many people believe that counselors primarily help people who are having problems. Although both of these assumptions are correct some of the time, they are not always accurate. For example, for the past several years, both small businesses and major corporations have come to realize that in running an effective business, their most valuable resources are their employees (Lewis & Lewis, 1986). Consequently, programs that address employees' needs for personal and professional development have proliferated. As a result of the increased demand for such programs, there has been an increased demand for people with skills in counseling to work in business and industry. Counselors who work in these settings do not always fill the traditional role of counseling people about their personal problems. This chapter addresses the diversified roles and responsibilities of counselors in business and industry.

The Beginning of a New Era

As World War II ended, 45 years ago, weary soldiers returned to the families and jobs they had left behind, bringing with them a serious problem. The stress of war had left its mark on some of these soldiers in the form of alcoholism or problem drinking. Many of these veterans were returning to jobs in plants and factories where the use of heavy equipment was a routine part of their work. Try to imagine an inebriated worker moving large tractors or working with dangerous machinery, such as an

61

acetylene welder, and you can begin to see the problem. These workers were not only endangering their own lives, but also the lives of their coworkers; and, if they were able to make it through the day without an accident, they were not very productive. Quickly, it became clear that something had to be done to decrease accidents and increase productivity. Companies all over America began to establish programs to assist employees with drinking problems (Dickman, Challenger, Emener, & Hutchison, 1988).

Employee Assistance Programs

Employee assistance programs (EAPs) today offer more services than ever before. The scope of EAP services has expanded to include marriage and family problems, financial concerns, drug-related problems (not just alcohol), legal concerns, and any other human problems or questions that might affect an employee's job performance.

Within the EAP field, there are two clearly defined jobs for counselors. First, there is the job of the EAP counselor and, second, there is the job of the EAP administrator. EAP counselors are available to assess employee problems or answer questions. EAP administrators oversee the program in its entirety.

EAP Counselors

EAP counselors meet with employees in a confidential setting to determine the nature of their concerns. Relationships between EAP counselors and employees are usually short-term and focus on problem assessment and referral to appropriate community resources. Referrals are made to a wide spectrum of community agencies including mental health centers, alcohol treatment centers, and credit counseling services, as well as to private practitioners such as attorneys, counselors, and psychologists.

It is important for EAP counselors to be current in their knowledge of these resources. They must understand the services different agencies provide, what costs are involved in the provision of these services, and the expertise of the professionals who deliver these services. The EAP counselor provides all this information to the employee in the counseling or assessment session. After the EAP counselor and employee have considered available resources, the counselor helps the employee contact the appropriate community resource. In sum, EAP counselors are professionals trained to listen to people's concerns, to assess the extent of their problems, and to assist them in getting the help they need to alleviate or cope with their problems.

In the past, EAP counselors were not trained professionally, but instead were recovering alcoholics (Dickman, et al.,1988). Although they had no formal training, they were well experienced with alcoholism and, therefore, could be very helpful to people who were struggling with this particular problem. Today, EAP counselors are not only trained professionally, usually holding a master's degree in counseling, social work, or psychology, but they can become certified as EAP specialists. To become a Certified Employee Assistance Professional (CEAP), one must have EAP experience and pass a written examination (see chapter 13). It should also be noted that most EAP counselors have had additional training in the field of substance abuse. Although the training is rigorous, the rewards are many. Most EAP counselors report that their work is challenging, highly variable, and offers adequate to comfortable financial rewards, with a beginning salary range of $25,000–$35,000.

EAP Administrators

The role of the EAP administrator is to coordinate the overall delivery of EAP services. This effort incorporates a wide range of responsibilities, beginning with program design. Each company's EAP is unique. It is imperative that EAPs match the specific needs of the organizations they serve, so EAP administrators generally spend considerable time with a company's personnel department to establish consistent policies and procedures for use of the EAP. Next, the EAP administrator conducts training sessions for employees and supervisors to describe the program and answer questions.

Throughout the life of the EAP, administrators must monitor and evaluate programs. EAP administrators prepare reports for companies to determine an EAP's use and effectiveness. They must also plan and carry out changes to enhance programs if reports indicate any degree of ineffectiveness.

Another ongoing task of the EAP administrator is to distribute program marketing materials. Effective EAPs are highly visible and are used frequently. Their degree of effectiveness is achieved through the dissemination of pamphlets, posters, and articles in company newspapers. All of these tasks fall under the responsibility of the EAP administrator. Finally, an EAP administrator is on call at all times to ensure that an EAP counselor is available, to attend to any program problems, and to serve as a liaison to company officials.

The work of EAP administrators is demanding, ever-changing, and requires great attention to detail. Whether the employing organization is large or small, the demands are the same. Typically EAP administrators are well experienced, attentive to details, have outgoing personalities, and do not mind erratic work schedules. They hold graduate degrees in counseling, social work, or psychology, many of them at a doctoral level. They have generally earned their CEAP. Beginning salaries for EAP administrators range from $35,000–$50,000.

EAP Professionals

EAP counselors and administrators may be employed within an organization as full-time employees, or outside the organization as consultants. EAP professionals within an organization are a part of an "internal" program and generally have offices in the personnel or medical department. EAP professionals who work outside the organization are part of an "external" program and generally have offices away from the organization.

Career Counseling

Vocational guidance was first introduced in this country by Frank Parsons at the beginning of the 20th century (Herr & Cramer, 1988). Parsons believed that adolescents needed some assistance in identifying their capabilities in order to choose the right job. Over the years, vocational guidance has evolved into career guidance and counseling, and its focus has expanded to include all ages of people and those who already have jobs (Herr, 1974).

Career Counselors

Career counselors occupy relatively new positions in business and industry. Their appearance in this setting may be directly correlated with a changing work force, new technology, and changes in society's attitude about quality of work life. For the past decade, major corporations have found that they must attend to employees' professional development on many levels. A critical demand has arisen to assist all employees in determining which job fits their personal and professional needs best.

Second, new technology has improved efficiency, but, in many cases, it has displaced employees from their jobs (Kuhlmann, 1988). Assembly-line workers who once routinely attached parts to pieces of machinery are being replaced by robots. Keypunch operators are being replaced by computers. Receptionists are being replaced by electronic telephone answering machines. Delivery persons are being replaced by electronic mail. Employees who perform these tasks are good workers who provide important services and who would like to continue to work, but where can they go in the organization if they are displaced by new technology?

Finally, the work ethic in America is changing. In the past, major corporations frequently asked their employees to pull up stakes and move on a regular basis. This practice might result in as many as 10 or 12 moves over the employee's life with the company. Until recently, nearly one in every five American families moved each year.

Today's employees are far less willing to relocate for their employer's convenience. They prefer to find other positions within the company that allow them to remain in their current location. Today's workers also seem more sensitive to finding a balance between work and family. Unlike the generations of workers that preceded them, they do not view work as the primary focus of their lives. Many of these employees are willing to adjust their careers within the organization to find a suitable position.

To help them in making such decisions, employees are using the services of career counselors. Corporations often hire full-time counselors to assist their employees in these efforts. In other cases, companies use the services of outside consultants. Career counselors work with employees to assess their skills, abilities, and interests and to explore career opportunities that fit these variables. Counselors obtain information from employees through interviews, tests, and employee self-exploration. The final decision about choice of career remains with the employee.

Career counselors generally hold a master's degree or a higher degree in counseling, social work, or psychology and have specialized training in career development. Many career counselors are certified as National Certified Career Counselors (NCCC) [see chapter 13]. To obtain this certification, one must have considerable experience and take a comprehensive written examination.

Beginning salaries are highly variable and seem to be influenced directly by whether the counselor is a full-time employee or an outside consultant. Career counselors who work for a specific corporation might begin at a salary of $25,000. Outside consultants, who typically charge as much as $100 per hour, could make considerably more money, depending on the number of hours spent in consulting.

Outplacement Counselors

Another specialty within the field of career counseling in business and industry is outplacement counseling. When employees are terminated, or entire plants or offices are closed, companies recognize that employees may need outplacement assistance because they may have limited job-seeking skills. Through training and personal counseling sessions, outplacement counselors give these employees the skills they need to find jobs, develop resumes, interview with confidence, and obtain new positions. Outplacement counselors have the same training as other career counselors, with a specialty in outplacement services. Their income is highly variable because it is determined by calculating a percentage of the salaries of the terminated employees.

Human Resources

Critical to the daily functioning of any organization is its human resources department. Generally, members of this department are concerned with the overall recruitment, development, management, and effectiveness of an organization's person power. The jobs within the field of human resources are highly variable and offer many employment possibilities to individuals who have had training in business, management, or many of the helping professions. In most small companies one person is responsible for the entire human resources operation. In larger companies the human resources department may list as many as 20 different job titles. What follows is a description of the major positions within the human resources field.

Employment Recruiters

Employment recruiters seek prospective employees and develop the means to attract them to their organizations. For example, if a company needs to hire new engineers, its employment recruiters will establish relationships with university engineering departments. Employment recruiters also establish close working relationships with human resources specialists in similar companies or related fields. Other responsibilities include the advertising of positions in professional or trade journals and newspapers, interaction with search firms and employment agencies, and the general release of information about job availability. An employment recruiter must arrange meetings with prospective candidates on an individual or a group basis. During these meetings, recruiters describe jobs more thoroughly than they might have in a journal ad and attempt to encourage candidates to meet with the company's employment interviewer.

Employment recruiters typically hold bachelor's degrees in business, management, psychology, or social work. Because it is frequently an entry-level position, this job requires little previous experience. It does, however, require high energy, an outgoing personality, and a willingness to travel. Beginning salaries range from $20,000–$25,000.

Employment Interviewers

Employment interviewers serve a vital role in the human resource department. Their first job is to discuss specific requirements for job vacancies with appropriate management personnel. Based on these discussions, they conduct screening interviews with prospective employees to determine whether a candidate's qualifications match the company's needs. The interview process also includes verifying a candidate's employment history, educational background, and references.

Employment interviewers typically make job offers to successful candidates and may negotiate salaries. They frequently conduct new employee orientations. They may also conduct exit interviews with employees who are leaving the company.

Educational preparation for this position usually includes a bachelor's degree in business, management, psychology, or social work. Interviewers generally have had some experience in other human resources areas before undertaking this position. It is helpful if the interviewer is warm and personable, attentive to detail, and does not mind working long hours during periods of corporate expansion or reduction. Beginning salaries range from $30,000–$35,000.

Employee Services Managers

Employee services managers establish, administer, and coordinate company-sponsored employee services. Specific tasks of this effort include coordinating the service awards program; arranging company-sponsored social activities; disseminating information and publications of interest to employees; assisting employees with relocation; participating in credit union activities; and supervising all employee recreation activities, including physical fitness and wellness programs.

This entry-level position is generally found only in large companies. The work can be exciting and challenging. Formal training requires a bachelor's degree in recreation, psychology, social work, or management. It is very important that individuals in this position have outgoing, positive personalities and are willing to work with many kinds of people in a variety of situations. Beginning salaries range from $18,000–$23,000.

Equal Employment Opportunity (EEO) Managers

EEO managers establish and implement corporate affirmative action/ equal employment opportunity programs. Their primary concern is that employees and potential employees be treated fairly and in compliance with government legislation and management's directives regardless of sex, age, race, ability, or veteran's status.

Specifically, EEO managers' responsibilities include establishing and monitoring EEO affirmative action programs for all segments of the company; reviewing company practices related to the hiring, training, transfer, and promotion of minority and female employees; analyzing job content to ensure that job titles and compensation are commensurate with work performed; investigating discrimination charges; developing a list from which female and minority candidates may be selected when jobs arise; ensuring that all tests used for hiring, promotion, or transfer have been evaluated professionally to eliminate bias; and keeping management apprised of changing governmental requirements.

Training for this position is highly variable. Some companies employ the services of attorneys whereas others use human resources specialists who hold, at least, a bachelor's degree in business, management, psychology, or social work. EEO managers must be knowledgeable and current with regard to government legislation and company policy. EEO managers must be assertive and comfortable with confrontation, because a routine part of their job is to address company errors. For attorneys, beginning salaries range from $80,000–$95,000. For individuals with bachelor's degrees and experience, salaries range from $35,000–$60,000.

Training Specialists

Training specialists are primarily concerned with the professional development of employees. Specific tasks include analyzing employee training needs, designing training programs, developing training manuals, purchasing and maintaining training equipment, and conducting training sessions.

Professionals in this field may work exclusively for the company in its training department, or be employed as outside consultants. Frequently, even companies that have "in-house" trainers hire outside trainers if they need a particular area of expertise to solve a given problem. In either case, training specialists are well educated and hold a doctoral or master's degree in business, management, counseling, psychology, or social work. Many trainers have had additional training in public speaking and effective communication. Salaries vary widely. It should simply be noted that trainers who work for a particular company receive a fixed salary, whereas outside trainers charge by the hour, day, or project. Training specialists must be current in their information, comfortable making presentations to groups of nearly any size, creative, and charismatic.

Human Resources Managers

The title of human resources manager is a relatively new one and replaces the old title of personnel manager. The primary function of a human resources manager is to oversee all programs and policies related to employees. Specific tasks include implementing established personnel policies; formulating and recommending new policies; overseeing employee recruitment, placement, and training; administering wage and salary policies; overseeing all labor-management functions; supervising the disbursement of benefits and compensation; and, generally overseeing all of the human resource functions that have been previously described in this chapter.

These professionals are highly experienced and generally hold bachelor's or master's degrees in business, management, counseling, psychology, or social work. Their salaries range from $50,000–$120,000 depending on the size of the company and the scope of their responsibilities. Their jobs are challenging and demanding and, therefore, require patience, tact, high energy, and creativity.

Organizational Consultants

Organizational consultants assess problems or concerns of a particular company and assist it in resolving these issues. Some specific examples of the types of concerns these consultants address include poor employee morale; low productivity; poor customer relations; and high employee turnover. They also assist in preparing for layoffs, downsizing, or expansion. Organizational consultants typically follow a three-step procedure. First, they assess the problem, which is generally accomplished by spending time at the company interviewing key personnel. Second, they make suggestions to management, both verbally and as a part of a written report. Third, they assist in implementing the changes through helping to create new policies, conducting training, or working with individual employees.

Unlike the jobs that were described previously, organizational consultants rarely work directly for the company that uses their services. Their work requires an ability to step back from the organization and see it without preconceived ideas. This is best done by someone who has no internal ties or personal relationships with the company's employees.

Organizational consultants are highly specialized and well trained. They often hold advanced graduate degrees in business, management, counseling, psychology, or social work. They have spent time working with companies in various capacities. Successful consultants are knowledgeable, competent, articulate, natural leaders, and tactful. This last trait is of particular importance, because the very nature of their work requires them to tell a company how to improve the way it is operating.

Organizational consultants charge by the hour, day, or project. Beginning salaries are variable, but consultants can earn from $50,000–$90,000.

A Growing Need

As America's factories and offices recognize the need for more humane work environments, the need for counselors, psychologists, and social workers will continue to grow. In some ways, these helping professionals are like all other helping professionals. In other ways, they are quite unique. A career in business and industry is not right for everyone, but for those who would find this work challenging, the door is wide open.

Further Information

You can find additional information about careers in business and industry from your counselor or career center. You might want to read those sections of the *Occupational Outlook Handbook* (OOH) that describe occupations mentioned in this chapter. The book by Lewis and Lewis (1986), listed in the References gives a good description of occupational skills and choices. Professional associations mentioned in this chapter are listed in the appendix. Addresses are provided so you can write for further information.

References

Dickman, F., Challenger, B.R., Emener, W.G., & Hutchison, W.S., Jr. (1988). *Employee assistance programs: A basic text*. Springfield, IL: Charles C Thomas.

Herr, E.L. (1974). *Vocational guidance and human development*. Boston: Houghton Mifflin.

Herr, E.L., & Cramer, S.H. (1988). *Career guidance and counseling through the life span*. Glenview, IL: Scott, Foresman.

Kühlmann, T.M. (1988). Adapting to technical change in the workplace. *Personnel Journal, 65*, 67–69.

Lewis, J.A, & Lewis, M.D. (1986). *Counseling programs for employees in the workplace*. Monterey, CA: Brooks/Cole.

Chapter 7

CAREERS IN PRIVATE PRACTICE

Burt Bertram

Private practice is an attractive option for many counseling and human development practitioners. In increasing numbers, counseling and human development practitioners are choosing to work as independent business people. Like physicians, lawyers, dentists, architects, and other professionals, counseling and human development practitioners establish offices in downtown or neighborhood professional office buildings where they offer their services to the general public. The professional and financial success of counseling and human development practitioners in private practice is dependent upon their ability to establish and build the reputation of their practice (business). In this way, the private practitioner is faced with a different challenge than is true for other practitioners. The private practitioner must be both a competent professional and a diligent manager of a business.

Structure of Private Practice

Practitioners may choose to establish either a limited (e.g., part-time) or a full-time private practice. Private practice can also be viewed as independent, nonsupervised practice. Counselors and human development professionals rarely go directly from graduate school into private practice. Licensing requirements as well as issues of practitioner competence usually dictate that the practitioner spend some number of years in institutional practice where there is the opportunity for ongoing formal supervision. Exceptions to this are when new practitioners affiliate with an existing private practitioner or private practice group.

Many practitioners begin their private practice on a part-time or limited basis while still fully employed within an institution, corporate setting, school, community agency, or other employment situation. This part-time practice can be established as an independent endeavor, but more often occurs in association with an established full-time private practitioner or group practice. Frequently the new professional uses a part-time private practice endeavor as a way to test the viability of private practice. Does the practitioner enjoy the freedom and responsibility of a small business? Does it seem that the practice can be successfully expanded to a full-time endeavor? Once the counselor or human development professional makes a decision regarding the long-term viability of private practice, the professional can then decide if he or she wishes to maintain a part-time endeavor or move into full-time private practice.

Some practitioners prefer to operate completely on their own and are referred to as sole practitioners. The alternative arrangement is to associate with others in a partnership or group practice arrangement. Sole practitioners work alone, sometimes with and sometimes without an office staff (reception/clerical). However, responsible sole practitioners do not operate in a professional vacuum—they develop a professional support system through local and national professional associations and develop colleague relationships with other members of the helping professions.

Practitioners frequently establish multidisciplinary partnerships or group practice relationships with social workers, psychologists, marriage and family therapists, and psychiatrists, as well as with other professional counselors or human development practitioners. Additionally, like the sole practitioner, responsible professionals in a partnership or group practice also establish support networks within professional associations and with members of other helping professions.

Focus of Practice

Private practice counselors and human development practitioners may have primary identification as counselors, consultants, or teacher-trainers. Some practitioners build their practice exclusively around one of these people-helping roles; however, most practitioners strike a balance among these and other people-helping roles. This clustering of roles occurs for several reasons. First, many practitioners choose private practice because of the opportunity for role diversity. Second, because private practitioners are self-employed, they usually are on the lookout for income-generating opportunities.

Counseling

Counseling is a confidential, therapeutic, and treatment-based relationship. Clients seek the assistance of a counselor to resolve some issue or concern in their life. Counseling, as a professional activity, covers a range of services and specific occupational titles. The occupational title used depends on state licensing requirements and the orientation and specialization of the practitioner. Terms such as *mental health counselor, licensed professional counselor, therapist, psychotherapist, marriage and family counselor, psychologist, social worker,* and *career counselor* are common titles for people providing counseling in private practice. Additionally, counselors sometimes further identify themselves by the use of speciality designations that include a wide range of terms defining or limiting the practitioner's interests or specialized skill. Speciality descriptions include titles like *child or adolescent counselor, rehabilitation counselor, substance abuse or addictions counselor, outplacement counselor, group counselor, gerontological counselor, divorce mediation counselor, hypnotherapist, eating disorders counselor,* and dozens more.

The actual practice of counseling in private practice is, in most ways, no different than the practice of counseling in a community agency, school, hospital, or treatment facility. The core responsibilities of the counselor remain the same. Counselors help people sort through and understand their problems and to take renewed control of their lives. The focus of counseling is on improving the client's response to the issues and dilemmas of life. As such, counselors in private practice know about and can respond to the issues and concerns of life—issues and concerns that exist throughout the life span from infancy to old age. Additionally, counselors are able to recognize and respond to the presence of abnormal or disturbed behaviors.

Counselors in private practice may establish a very general practice wherein they therapeutically respond to almost any human issue or concern from preschool children to issues of death and dying; however, most private practitioners specialize or limit their practice to certain types of client problems. As an example, many counselors principally work with children or adolescents, others focus on issues of adults or older persons, and still others prefer to concentrate on relationship issues between spouses, family members, or other personal or business relationships. Another way that counselors specialize is based on the presenting problem of the client. Such concerns as substance abuse, physical or sexual abuse, illness or injury rehabilitation, academic or learning problems, eating disorders, stress/anxiety or panic disorders, career and employability concerns, or mid-life crises are but a few examples of presenting-problem specializations.

Consulting

Consulting is a supervisory or advising-based relationship. The consultant possesses certain skills or expertise the client desires. The consultant-client relationship, unlike the counselor-client relationship, is not therapeutic or treatment-based. Consulting is an activity for the seasoned, experienced practitioner.

Consulting in the people-helping professions is an activity that covers a wide range of services and specific occupational titles. Consulting titles tend to reflect the setting or purpose of the consulting relationship. Examples of consulting titles include program consultants, gerontological consultants, learning consultants, parenting or child raising consultants, human relations consultants, organizational development consultants, and management development consultants. The practice of consulting can be thought of as occurring in three different forms—supervisory consulting, expert consulting, and process consulting.

Supervisory consulting. Supervisory consultants are retained by a people-helping organization (i.e., school, treatment facility, hospital, community agency, etc.) in order to provide technical supervision (critique, assistance, advice) to the professional staff within the organization. An example of this type of consulting relationship would involve a counselor providing technical supervision to the counseling staff of an agency, school, or treatment facility regarding effective counseling strategies for a particular client. Another example would be when a human development professional, expert in issues of services to the aging, would provide technical consultation to the staff of a nursing home or rehabilitation center.

Expert consulting. Expert consultants may be retained by organizations or may offer their expertise directly to individuals through in-office consultation sessions. Counselors and human development professionals often develop specific expertise in areas of student personnel services and learning capabilities testing, diagnosis, and treatment, whereas others serve as expert consultants to parent-child education programs. Another example of expert consulting would be when the practitioner serves as a court-appointed evaluator or expert witness for everything from child custody to criminal rehabilitation. Every phase of human experience is a potential area of expert consulting for the counselor and human development professional.

Process consulting. Process consulting involves assisting groups of people or organizations to understand, change, or control the attitudes or behaviors of the group or organization. Process consultants are frequently referred to as human relations consultants, organization development consultants, or management consultants. Process consultants work with group members on issues of communication, leadership, trust, teamwork, cooperation, respect, and productivity that affect the activities or performance of the group.

Teaching-Training

Counselors and human development professionals are always in the process of teaching and training. Usually these activities occur informally through the counseling or consulting experience. Frequently, however, practitioners have the opportunity to engage in formal classroom teaching or training as members of counselor education departments. Counselor educators teach counseling and human development courses in colleges, universities, and adult education programs. Additionally, practitioners are called upon by businesses, associations, and community agencies to provide skill training programs on topics such as effective listening, assertive communication, conflict resolution, and stress management.

Teaching and training provide practitioners with marketing and public relations opportunities for their practice, as well as enhanced income and a way to balance the intense one-on-one personal nature of counseling and human development services. In addition to counseling, consulting, and teaching-training, some private practitioners supplement their practice with professional speaking and writing as well as producing people-helping materials (books, tapes, videos).

Education-Certification-Licensing Requirements

For an activity such as counseling and human development services to become a profession, there must be clearly recognized standards of preparation and experience that ensure practitioner competence. These criteria define when practitioners are ready to offer their professional services to the general public. The guidance for these standards comes from three primary sources—professional associations like the American Association for Counseling and Development (AACD), the American Psychological Association (APA), the National Association of Social Work (NASW), or the American Association for Marriage and Family Therapy (AAMFT); senior faculty members from colleges and universities who prepare practitioners; and from state legislative bodies that pass licensing legislation. These three sources combine to define who may and who may not engage in the private practice of counseling and human development services.

Education. The private practice of counseling and human development requires (by state license) or recommends (professional associations and university faculty) that practitioners hold a master's or doctoral degree in counseling or another human service discipline. There is no single best undergraduate (bachelor's) degree that prepares a student for a master's or doctoral program in counseling. Bachelors degrees in education, sociology, psychology, anthropology, the humanities, political science, health, literature, and theology are common backgrounds for future private practitioners. The important thing is to learn all you can about the human experience, about the ups and downs of life, so you have a grasp of the whole person—body, mind, and soul.

Currently many graduate-level counselor education programs are participating in a voluntary accreditation process especially designed for the general preparation of counselors and human development professionals. When evaluating counselor education graduate programs, look for the appropriate accreditation (Hollis & Wantz, 1986) [see chapter 13].

When considering a master's or doctoral program it is as important for you, the prospective student, to interview members of the faculty as it is for them to interview you. Talk with the faculty about accreditation as well as other special issues that are important to you. Ask them how their program meets accreditation standards, and learn about their philosophy and practice of counseling. Finally, counselor preparation is a strongly values-based experience. Successful counselor preparation largely depends on a compatible match between student and program philosophy. Do your homework. Your decision will shape the foundation of your career. The knowledge, skills, and values you learn in your master's or doctoral program will provide the structure for your professional identity and competence.

Certification. Certification of counselors and human development professionals is an evaluation process based on education, experience, examination, and professional recommendation. Practitioners are certified by recognized and accepted certifying organizations as meeting the standards necessary for the general practice of counseling or for specialist designation. Practitioners in private practice are especially mindful of and responsive to certification opportunities. Certification serves as a marketable credential that attests to the professional competence of the practitioner. The primary counselor certification designations include the following (see also chapter 13):

- Nationally Certified Counselor (NCC)
- Certified Rehabilitation Counselor (CRC)
- Clinical Member, American Association for Marriage and Family Therapy (AAMFT)
- Certified Clinical Mental Health Counselor (CCMHC)

The primary psychologist certification descriptions include:

- National Register of Health Care Providers
- Diplomate of the American Board of Professional Psychology

The primary social worker certification designation is:

- American Society of Clinical Social Work

Other speciality certifications are currently being discussed or established. Practitioners, both in private practice and institutionally employed, will want to apply for certification in their speciality areas as certification becomes available.

Licensing requirements. Increasingly the private practice of counseling, and to a lesser degree human development services, has become regulated or licensed by individual state legislatures. Licensing of professional counselors is especially important for all practicing counselors and especially for privately practicing counselors. Licensing helps regulate the practice of counseling by preventing well-intentioned but untrained persons from practicing. Additionally, licensing often assists the practitioner to qualify for the receipt of health insurance reimbursement for counseling and human development services.

Currently 32 states define who may and who may not engage in the private practice of counseling and some human development services. Efforts within state legislative bodies are currently under way to establish counselor licensing laws in every state.

Frequently there is a link between certification and licensing. Many states use the National Board for Certified Counselors (NBCC) examination as the basis for the state licensure exam. This trend of using the standards and certification examination from both general and speciality credentialing agencies is expected to continue.

Personal Characteristics

The common denominator of all counselors and human development professionals involves an enduring fascination and respect for human life. Although there are many exceptions to the rule, practitioners, both in private practice and institutionally employed, tend to have certain personality characteristics in common. To be effective, counselors must be able to work with many different types of people. Therefore, counselors need to have a high tolerance for individual differences and be able to be objective about people and life-styles.

Counseling is both art and science. Successful practitioners thoroughly develop and constantly upgrade their technical competence. At the same time, most successful counselors have a unique, perhaps even intuitive, personal touch to their counseling practice. It is this very human, person-to-person ability, when combined with rigorous professional training, that creates the essence of the counseling experience.

Counseling work is rarely simple or straightforward. Counselors and human development professionals encounter people during times of distress and crisis. During these stressful times clients rarely think or behave logically; therefore, practitioners must have a well-developed tolerance for ambiguity and uncertainty. Individual change in people takes time and does not move forward in a straight line. Counselors must blend gentle patience with firm confrontation as they guide clients through difficult times. Successful counselors know when to push and when to back off. And always, counselors must know how to convey a sense of warmth and respect to clients that communicates a strong belief in their ability to make their own decisions and take charge of their own lives.

In addition to these general counselor characteristics, unique personal characteristics are required of the successful private practitioner. Private practitioners must possess special characteristics related to the development and management of a small business. These business-person characteristics begin with the acceptance that success or failure depends only on you. Everything that occurs or fails to occur in your practice is your responsibility. As with all things, there is a tension between the exhilaration of being your own boss and the 24-hour, 7-day-per-week reality of knowing that you are responsible for your own success. Successful private practitioners must be self-starters. They must be people who can define for themselves what needs to be done and then do it themselves, or see to it that it is accomplished by someone.

Private practice, like any business, is either growing or declining. Private practitioners must be willing and able constantly to market their counseling business by seeking opportunities for community visibility, contacting new referral sources, and maintaining effective working relationships with existing referral sources. The ability to sell oneself as competent and caring is critical to success in private practice.

In private practice, money is always an issue. Practitioners must be able to decide comfortably what their time is worth based on their experience, education, and the norms of the community. Is their time worth $35 per hour? $50 per hour? $75 per hour? or $100+ per hour? Can the practitioner comfortably and professionally state a fee and then assertively, without apology, collect the fee? Can the practitioner negotiate with consulting or teaching clients and institutions regarding services and fees?

Managing the business side of the practice includes setting up and maintaining an office space, paying the bills, and managing employees. It also involves remaining current and responding to ever-changing licensing, insurance, and taxation laws that affect you and your employees.

Another critical personal characteristic relates to the practitioner's comfort with income ups and downs. Most private practitioners eventually arrive at a fairly steady income level, but even for veteran practitioners there are lean times when circumstances conspire to reduce income dramatically. How critical is it to you and your family that you have a guaranteed paycheck? Do you have the discipline to save for that inevitable lean time when your practice is slow—when your income is reduced but your business and living expenses remain?

Private practice is time- and energy-intensive. Are you prepared to work as long and hard as it takes to make your practice become what you want? Many practitioners work 50–70 hours per week to establish their practice and then nearly as many when the practice becomes successful. Unlike working for an institution, there are no predetermined working hours, days on, or days off. To regulate your work schedule you simply must listen to the voice within to determine when the job is done for the day or the week. Paid vacations, paid sick days, and retirement accounts are never guaranteed for the private practitioner. Everything depends on you and the success of your practice.

Finally, private practice, especially full-time private practice, is a risk. It is a risk that involves a substantial investment of financial and ego resources. People who are uncomfortable taking risks might want to consider whether the stability of institutional employment would not outweigh the uncertainties and ambiguities of private practice.

Income From Private Practice

Income varies with every practitioner. Part-time practitioners usually supplement their regular institutional salary. Once established, net income (after business expenses) from a part-time practice can range from an average of $75 to $250 per week.

Net income from an established full-time practice can range from $25,000 to $100,000 per year depending on the drive, determination, clinical competence, and business skills of the practitioner. In a recent survey conducted by the Psychotherapy Finances (1988), full-time private counseling practitioners reported an average annual net income of $40,929 for women and $46,070 for men. Net income is ultimately a product of the efforts of the practitioner factored into the economic, legal, and competitive conditions within a given geographic area.

Is Private Practice for You?

To review, private practice is an exciting, self-dependent, and self-motivated career opportunity within the counseling and human development professions. However, private practice may not be for everyone. Private practice is generally considered to be independent practice. Therefore, most private practitioners tend to be experienced, well-established professionals. Private practitioners normally hold a master's or doctoral degree in counseling, psychology, social work, or another human service discipline.

A private practice can be developed as a full- or part-time endeavor and may or may not include affiliation with partners. Some practitioners prefer to develop a sole practice. Private practitioners often develop a practice that is a blend of several occupational roles. It is not uncommon for the private practitioner to engage in many different counseling, consulting, and teaching-training endeavors.

More then 30 states have counselor licensure; all 50 states and the District of Columbia require psychologists to be licensed. Practitioners are encouraged to obtain certification designations that attest to their qualification for independent or speciality practice. The trend toward speciality certification and state licensing is expected to continue.

When evaluating the suitability of private practice, special consideration should be given to the unique demands of small business ownership. The successful private practitioner must be both a competent professional and a diligent manager of a business. Private practice is a risk. If you enjoy independence, are not frightened by the normal ups and downs of business, get excited about the opportunity to create something for yourself, and are willing to dedicate the time, energy, and resources necessary, private practice may be a risk that is just right for you.

Further Information

You can obtain additional information about private practice in counseling from the following professional associations whose addresses are listed in the appendix:

American Mental Health Counselors Association
American Association for Counseling and Development
American Psychological Association
American Association for Marriage and Family Therapy
National Association for Social Work

References

Hollis, J., & Wantz, R. (1986). *Counselor preparation 1986–1989.* Muncie, IN: Accelerated Development.

Psychotherapy Finances. (1988). *Fee & practice survey 1988.* Hawthorne, NJ: Ridgewood Financial Institute.

Chapter 8

CAREERS IN PUBLIC AND PRIVATE AGENCIES

Robert A. Male

The information presented in this chapter focuses on the nature and types of counseling and related human development occupations that exist in public and private agencies. There is considerable diversity in the counseling profession. This diversity is readily apparent in the differences among community-based public and private agencies. It is not possible to include information on all types of agencies that provide counseling services, so the focus of this chapter will be on the most common types of agencies that provide direct and indirect services to the communities they represent and serve. The agencies, services, and occupational information presented in this chapter are generic and generalized representations of the type of situation one would be likely to find when exploring community-based agencies.

Community-based public and private agencies exist primarily to meet the needs and mandates of the community they serve. Each agency is a functioning system that operates in accord with other systems. Just as each person is unique and different (and a functioning system), each counselor, agency, and community is unique and functions to fulfill specific mandates and missions. Operationally, each agency receives its funding from a variety of sources. This is one factor that influences the type of client served, the nature and number of counselors or human development professionals on its staff, and other factors such as work setting and salary ranges. Three types of agencies will be presented here: public agencies, private nonprofit agencies, and private for-profit agencies.

Public Agencies

Community-based public agencies are those whose major portion of funding is usually provided by the county or the municipal government.

The persons who work at these agencies are most often employees of the sponsoring county or municipality.

County Mental Health Programs

An example of such an agency is a county mental health program that serves a community (county population). The services a county mental health services agency (CMHS) provides are usually delivered at a centralized location operated similarly to a counseling center. There is a reception area and offices for counselors to provide individual counseling, and larger rooms for group counseling and educational presentations.

Community Mental Health Services (CMHS) often have people working primarily in one location to provide professional mental health services to the community. The persons working at such an agency are almost exclusively professionally trained, with advanced degrees and professional experience. For example, in a staff of 70, there might be four psychiatrists (MDs with a specialization in psychiatry), 15 doctoral-level clinical or counseling psychologists, six nurse practitioners possessing master's degrees in nursing with an emphasis in psychiatry or psychology, 40 counselors with master's degrees in either counseling or social work, and 5 psychiatric/mental health aides possessing bachelor's degrees in psychology or a related human services field. In addition to having achieved the degrees listed, professional staff members of this type of agency also usually have additional specialized training and experience in the focal service delivery areas of the agency. Agencies also employ support staff to take care of reception and clerical responsibilities.

The job titles of public employees are often organized along civil service lines. For example, master's level counselors and nurse practitioners may have a job classification of Mental Health Specialist. In addition, the counselor's level of education, training, experience, and duration of employment is represented by an additional classification of I, II, or III. In the CMHS an entry-level counselor with a master's degree and a minimum of experience would be classified as a Mental Health Specialist I, whereas the most highly trained and experienced counselor would be classified as a Mental Health Specialist III. Psychiatrists maintain the discreteness of their job title but may be classified as a Psychiatrist (entry level) or Senior Psychiatrist. Psychologists also may be classified as a Psychologist I (newly graduated, nonlicensed psychologist) up through Psychologist II or Senior Psychologist (the most experienced). The job classification of bachelor's degree professional staff may be Psychiatric Aide or Mental Health Aide. The master's-level nurse or nurse practitioner is frequently classified with the other master's-degree-level staff as a Mental Health Specialist.

The job responsibilities of the professional staff are often defined by the mission, mandate, and clientele of the employing agency. As an example, a CMHS agency may have a primary mandate to provide services to the mentally and emotionally disturbed persons in the community. Thus, the primary responsibility of the professional staff is to help severely disturbed, depressed, anxious, and psychotic individuals as well as attempting to provide necessary mental health services to other members of the community. Public agencies provide services to a broad section of the community; however, the current trend, due to shrinking or fixed resources and a growing population, seems to be to provide services to only the most severely disturbed people and to refer those with lesser problems to private agencies.

In addition to serving the mentally and emotionally disturbed population, a CMHS may also have a program for children providing group, individual, and play therapy to children and families, and an alcohol and substance abuse program involving educational and treatment programs. Many of the clients who come to this type of agency do so on court mandate. Others are clients because they have serious problems and lack the resources to get alternate types of help. Thus, the clients of public agencies are often lower income individuals, families, and children who are in need of mental health services but lack the personal resources to secure help on their own. Professionals working at a CMHS are frequently involved in intake interviews, assessment, therapeutic service delivery, and referral to hospitals of persons considered psychotic or severely disturbed and at risk. The type of client and the agency's mission play a large role in determining the personal characteristics of the staff that are best suited to working in this setting.

The job responsibilities as noted include intake consultations and assessments, psychological and behavioral assessments, individual counseling/therapy, family or group counseling/therapy, referral, and educational/behavioral program instruction (e.g., substance abuse, AIDS, stress management, and self-help). These responsibilities are completed either by an individual practitioner with responsibility for the management and control of a particular case, or by a team that might include a psychiatrist, a psychologist, an aide, and other team members. A professional working in this environment should be able to diagnose problems and provide appropriate therapeutic intervention. In addition, professionals who work in public agencies should be psychologically and emotionally prepared to deal with many of the most difficult, frustrating, and sometimes unresolvable problems helping professionals confront. Support and supervision are provided, but counselors must be prepared to look after their own well-being and develop mechanisms to guard against burnout.

Most of the service delivery in a CMHS is diagnostic and therapeutic in nature. Nearly all the professional staff would be considered clinicians.

Typical funding of a CMHS comes from federal and state sources through allocations to the county. The agency will also receive third party payments for services rendered to clients who are covered by insurance. Public agencies occasionally secure grants from private and public sources to operate specific programs for members of their community. The funding of such agencies may vary somewhat from year to year with the primary sponsor, in this case a county, assuming primary responsibility for maintaining a funding level sufficient to support the work site and staffing levels.

Counselors and human development professionals hired for public agencies are typically required to be eligible to obtain certification and/or licensure consistent with their position. For example, psychiatrists and psychologists would be expected to be licensed (e.g., licensed clinical psychologist). Social workers are typically required to be registered or licensed (e.g., licensed clinical social worker). Counselor certification and licensure is becoming more prevalent nationally, and if licensure exists in a given state, then one would normally be expected to be a licensed professional counselor in order to be hired by a public agency. National certifications might also be required of counselors, such as Nationally Certified Counselor (NCC) or Certified Clinical Mental Health Counselor (CCMHC) [see chapter 13].

Employment at most public agencies as a professional service provider requires at least a bachelor's degree in order to secure a position as a Mental Health Aide/Psychiatric Aide. Wages for this position start at $5.00 per hour or $10,500 per year at entry and may range as high as $24,000 per year for a Senior Aide. The wage range for a counselor, social worker, or nurse with a master's degree and experience is $19,200 per year at entry and rises to $42,000 per year for senior staff. In a civil service system, a Mental Health Specialist I may earn between $18,000 to $25,200 per year; a Mental Health Specialist II might earn between $26,400 to $34,800 per year; and, a Mental Health Specialist III might earn between $36,000 to $42,000 per year. Mental health nurses generally enter a public agency as a Mental Health Specialist II or III. Staff psychologists have a PhD in clinical or counseling psychology and may enter a public agency at a wage of $28,800 per year, eventually earning a top wage in the neighborhood of $48,000 per year. Staff psychiatrists may start at a wage of $60,000 per year and progress to earn as much as $84,000–$96,000 per year.

In addition to the wages described, fringe benefits such as health and dental insurance plans and contributions to retirement programs may increase the compensation realized by public employees by as much as 15%. Managerial positions within a public agency provide additional compensation. A public agency may have both a Clinical Director and an Administrative Director. The Clinical Director is responsible for the delivery of all clinical services. The Administrative Director is responsible for the management of financial resources, support services, and facilities. The Clinical Director is typically an experienced professional with a PhD degree in counseling or psychology. The Agency Administrator most frequently has experience, education, and training in the areas of business and management. The Clinical Director of a CMHS might earn between $40,000–$60,000 per year.

County Youth Programs

Other types of public agencies also exist, such as County Youth Programs. A County Youth Program (CYP) in a smaller rural county than the CMHS above may be smaller in number of staff—including Counselor IIs with master's degrees in counseling, and Counselor Is with bachelor's degrees (perhaps one in drug and alcohol counseling and one in corrections). Such a CYP might be financed by state funds distributed through the county financial system. The Clinical Director might be a counselor with a master's degree, hold a job classification of "Counselor II," and earn a wage that may reach $30,000 per year. A Counselor I on the same staff might have only a bachelor's degree and make $19,200 per year to start. County employees usually get fringe benefits and some extra wages for management (though not always). This kind of CYP also could have a position of Program Director who is responsible for the service delivery of a particular program.

The clients of a CYP could be children and adolescents who are wards of the state, have been placed in foster homes, or have been referred by the State Children's Services Division as needing help. The biological parents and foster parents may also be clients. Service delivery might include intake interviews, assessments, individual and group or family counseling, educational programs, and referral. Counselors work with clients in the home, school, and their agency's offices. Foster parents might receive training from the agency before placement of a child by the Program Coordinator.

Information on the requirements, wages, and availability of counseling positions in public agencies is most readily obtained in the employment section of newspapers or directly from the personnel departments of counties and municipalities providing the services. One should keep in mind that the types of services provided, wages of the professional staff, and mandated missions of the agency all vary with the location of the community being served. For example, one would not expect the same wage range for a counseling position in a public agency in Los Angeles County, California, and Chittenden County, Vermont.

Private Nonprofit Agencies

Private nonprofit agencies probably account for the greatest diversity in services, wages, and vocational opportunities in the counseling profession. Community-based nonprofit agencies receive their funding from a wide variety of sources. Persons who work at these agencies are employees of the agency itself. Examples of agencies of this type include religiously affiliated counseling service centers such as Catholic Family Services and Jewish Family & Child Services, and nonaffiliated agencies serving specific elements of communities such as the aged, the homeless, or adolescent runaways.

Family and Child Services Agencies

An example of this type of agency might be a religiously affiliated family and child services center. The services provided by a Family & Child Services (FCS) agency are intended to be consistent with the mission—for example, to provide quality mental health services to persons regardless of religious affiliation. Typically, religion plays little role in the acceptance of clients for treatment or in the type of treatment administered. An FCS is operated along the lines of a traditional counseling center, with most of the services being provided at one location with facilities for individual, family, and group counseling. When possible, such an agency also has a space large enough to allow for educational programs.

An FCS might have several full-time staff counselors, all of whom have master's degrees in counseling or social work with additional professional experience. Agencies such as this do not normally employ mental health aides as the client group is usually not as severely disturbed as those treated at a public mental health agency or hospital. In this type of agency, counselors usually assume full responsibility for the client's services, with some ongoing supervision by the clinical director. The counselor's responsibility with the client normally begins at the intake interview and is carried on through assessment and therapeutic service delivery to case closure or referral. Depending on the size of the agency, some specialists may have expertise in particular treatment methods for problems such as eating disorders or substance abuse. If such a situation exists, then a counselor who does an intake interview may refer a client to an in-house specialist for a particular type of assistance. It is also possible that two counselors might colead groups or cocounsel with a family or couple. This type of service delivery is often used as a way to increase counseling skills and receive supervision and feedback from a colleague.

An FCS employs support staff as needed to take care of reception and clerical responsibilities.

There is rarely any distinction in titles with the employees of a private agency except when a counselor takes on a managerial responsibility, such as that of clinical director. The clinical director of a nonprofit agency might be a licensed clinical social worker (LCSW) with a master's degree. The rest of the staff could be evenly distributed among those with master's degrees in counseling, psychology, and social work.

The clients served at such an agency vary with the agency's mandate and mission. An agency may function primarily as a counseling center dealing with the full range of individual and family difficulties such as depression, posttraumatic stress disorder, grief and loss, or separation and divorce. Counselors employed by such agencies are normally generalists with expertise in and knowledge of counseling theory and techniques but not necessarily possessing skills in the area of diagnosis of mental illness. Clients requiring medication, or whose difficulties are beyond the scope of the agency's resources, are referred for treatment elsewhere. Chronically mentally ill clients may receive ongoing counseling services at an agency such as this if the agency's staff can meet their needs.

In addition, an FCS may have programs to meet the needs of specialized populations within the community. Examples of these types of programs are homemaker services for the aged and housebound; homemaker services for young, inexperienced parents; immigrant/refugee relocation and counseling services; and a wide variety of community educational and self-help programs.

Job responsibilities include intake interviews with available counselors being assigned clients, case planning, individual counseling, family or group counseling, and educational/behavioral instruction or referral. The counselor providing services receives periodic supervision and consultation from the clinical director. Counselors working in this environment should be well grounded ethically, knowledgeable and experienced in counseling theory and technique, and self-sufficient with regard to professional development and protecting themselves from burnout.

Funding of a religiously affiliated agency comes from a number of sources, including United Way and other charities, private contributors, direct payments from clients and health insurance companies, program fees, sponsorship from the religious charities, grants (federal, state, county, etc.), and contracts with other agencies such as Children's Services Divisions and schools. Agency administration is frequently divided: The executive director looks after operational costs and the financial administration of the agency, and the clinical director is responsible for the quality of service delivery. The wage range for a counselor with a master's degree at such an agency is from $16,000 per year to $28,000 per year for full-time employment. Some agencies employ part-time counselors on an hourly basis at a wage ranging from $8–$15 per hour. Agency funding may vary from year to year—this may have a significant impact on the number of staff positions and the wages provided.

Counselors working for a nonprofit community agency may need to be credentialed or certified in addition to possessing the appropriate education and experience. At present, there do not seem to be any uniform criteria, but the trend is for counselors to be state licensed if licensure exists, and for counselors to be appropriately certified (e.g., NCC, CCMHC) [see chapter 13]. In a competitive job market, the person who is licensed or certified has an advantage in applying for open positions. The primary source of information about job openings in nonprofit agencies is the employment section of local newspapers. College and university counseling programs and national, state, and local counseling organizations may also be useful sources of information.

Special Need Agencies and Programs

Many other types of private nonprofit community agencies exist. These agencies are often created to meet specific needs in the community. They include programs for sheltering and meeting the needs of adolescent runaways; mentally retarded or developmentally disabled adolescents and adults; or the aged or homeless who are incapable of meeting their own needs without assistance.

Requirements for employment and the wages that might be paid at special need agencies are usually lower than those in the other agencies described. The highest paid individual would ordinarily be the clinical supervisor or program supervisor. The clinical supervisor has managerial responsibility as well as direct service delivery responsibilities and may earn up to $30,000 per year. Clinical supervisors most often have a master's degree in counseling, counseling psychology, social work, or special education with considerable experience in the field. Staff counselors will normally have master's degrees and earn between $15,000–$22,000 per year. Program coordinators, or those with specialized tasks and responsibilities, may earn between $18,000–$25,000 per year.

Agencies such as these may have other persons on the staff with much less training who deliver services. For example, it would not be unusual to have nondegreed persons serving as crisis specialists on either a volunteer or hourly wage basis. If the agency has a residential facility serving as a halfway house, it might also have peer counselors or residential supervisors employed for room and board and a stipend. There is considerable variety in the education, experience, and background of the paraprofessional staff of an agency such as this. Normally, paraprofessional staff receive on-site training and supervision from the agency's professional staff and assume service delivery responsibilities when considered sufficiently educated. These types of private agencies provide the greatest programmatic diversity and perhaps the greatest opportunity for entry-level counselors to secure a job and gain experience (see chapter 12).

Private For-Profit Agencies

Private practice counseling agencies that are created to make a profit for the owners differ in many respects from nonprofit agencies. Structurally, for-profit agencies are often incorporated and have an active board of directors who provide operational and fiscal direction to the agency. Service delivery ranges from individual counseling for a fee (self or insurance paid) to large-scale programs such as employee assistance programs (see chapter 6) under contracts to large companies. An agency such as this hires counselors who are generalists as well as those with specific education, training, and experience. These agencies exist in a very competitive environment with marketing playing a much larger role than is the case with nonprofit agencies. Because specific information about this type of agency is obtainable elsewhere in this volume (see chapter 7), no attempt will be made to elaborate further here.

In summary, considerable and diverse possibilities exist for persons wishing to be counselors in a public or private agency. A counselor's access to the job market and wages depends on education, training, interests, experience, and location. Wages start at minimum wage for paraprofessionals and rise to annual wages in excess of $40,000.

Further Information

Additional insight into the field of community counseling can be found in the following reference: Lewis J.A., & Lewis, M.D. (1989). *Community counseling*. Pacific Grove, CA: Brooks/Cole. You could also talk with your counselor about this field of work, or you could write any of the following associations for information:

American Association for Counseling and Development
American Mental Health Counseling Association
American Rehabilitation Counseling Association
American Psychological Association
National Association for Social Work

Chapter 9

CAREERS IN FEDERAL AND STATE AGENCIES

Andrew A. Helwig

Many counseling and human development occupations are found in state and federally funded agencies. Many state agencies such as vocational rehabilitation, public employment service (Job Service), and other employment and training programs falling under the Job Training Partnership Act (JTPA) are, in fact, funded partially or completely by federal dollars. Although many state and federal agencies have no positions such as counselor, a vast number do.

Employment counseling and vocational rehabilitation counseling employ large numbers of workers. Because the field of corrections is rapidly growing, the occupations of correction psychologist, correction counselor, parole officer, and youth counselor are explained. Finally, the less well-known occupation of military counselor is presented.

Dozens of other counselor and human development occupations exist at federal, state, or municipal governmental levels. Some of these are long-standing occupations such as counseling and clinical psychologist (principally at Veterans Affairs facilities and state hospitals) and social worker. Other occupations are psychiatric technician or aide, drug and alcohol treatment specialist, job placement specialist, developmental disabilities specialist, veterans' counselor, psychological services associate, and the more generic occupations of human services worker and mental health worker. Newer occupations funded by some governmental units include victim's advocate, independent adoptions specialist, and aging services representative.

Employment Counselor

Places to Work

Employment counselors typically work for the Job Service, which is the public employment service in the United States. In most cases, the employment counselor is a state employee. Some employment counselors who work for government agencies may be county or city employees.

Employment counselors may work in small rural community offices or large metropolitan offices with over 100 workers. There are over 2,000 state employment offices throughout the country, although not all of them have employment counselors. Individuals who do employment counseling may be called vocational or career counselors, Job Service Representatives, Job Service Specialists, or by some other title.

Colleagues at Work

The employment counselor works with a number of other professional staff persons. Most state employment offices have employment or placement interviewers. There may also be workers specializing in employment services to veterans; these workers have titles such as veterans employment service representative or disabled veteran outreach program specialist. In some Job Service offices applicants can file for unemployment insurance following layoff or job termination. In such offices, the employment counselor would also have contact with unemployment insurance claims representatives.

Whom Would You Help?

The range of applicants (clients) seeking employment counseling in state employment agencies is extremely wide. It might be a 14-year-old youth seeking an after-school or summer job. It could be a 17-year-old dropout facing juvenile detention if he doesn't find work. It could be a 36-year-old unemployed woman in the process of divorce and anxious about supporting herself and her children. It might be a 52-year-old man terminated from a job after 25 years because a factory is closing. It may be a 72-year-old who is sick of retirement but needs help transferring her skills to a new job.

Employment counseling has traditionally been defined as assisting clients with problems of occupational choice, change, or adjustment. Clients may be young or old, from all socioeconomic levels, and of all racial and ethnic groups. Perhaps because state employment agencies charge no fees for services provided, clients are typically of lower socioeconomic levels. Other clients such as recent college graduates, military retirees, and mid-career changers also use the Job Service. Not many other counselor groups are able to work with as broad a range of clients as the employment counselor.

Job Responsibilities

Employment counselors assist people in choosing an occupation, changing a career, or adjusting to a work environment. A helping relationship must be established so the client and counselor can accurately assess the situation. Formal assessment techniques such as aptitude and interest inventories might be used. If a career choice or change decision is to be made, the employment counselor needs to bring an assortment of information to the counseling process. This information may include local and state labor market information such as occupational trends and job demands. Information about employers may be helpful. Sometimes information about training opportunities, including vocational/technical programs and private schools or colleges, is needed as well as admission requirements and financial aid data.

In other instances, employment counselors may work with clients who have multiple barriers to employment. Clients may have a poor work history, lack skills, have a history of drug or alcohol abuse, or have personality characteristics that hinder them from finding or keeping a job. With such a client, the employment counselor may develop a plan to confront employability barriers. Supportive services from other community agencies are necessary to deal with some of the identified barriers to employment. Knowledge of community resources and the ability to work cooperatively with such agencies is critical. The employment counselor may work as a case manager ensuring that a variety of services is provided the client.

The employment counselor may also be responsible for increasing the employability of clients by providing job-seeking skills workshops. Completing work applications, writing resumes, and preparing for job interviews may be the focus of such group activities. Employment counselors may also work with employers and refer counseled applicants to job openings.

Personal Characteristics

Employment counselors must relate to and establish relationships with a broad range of clients. They should be sensitive to and understand individual differences. They must understand human behavior, both positive and negative. Employment counselors should be flexible, patient, and able to handle frustrations due to working with difficult clients, poor working conditions, or assignment of noncounseling duties. Tolerance for administrative procedures and record keeping is helpful.

Education and Training

States have considerable autonomy regarding the education and experience requirements of applicants for employment counselor positions. Substituting related work experience for some educational requirements is often possible. Consequently, some entry-level employment counselor positions may be filled by individuals with a bachelor's degree or less. The educational standard for a journeyman employment counselor, as specified by the profession, is a master's degree in counseling or a closely related field.

Salary

Yearly starting salaries for employment counselors who work for state employment agencies range from $18,000 to $25,000. In cities or in county government agencies the lower end of the range may be $13,000.

Correction Psychologist and Correction Counselor

Places to Work

Psychologists and counselors employed in corrections are likely to work in state and federal prisons; these institutions are characterized as maximum, medium, or minimum in security requirements. Facilities housing juvenile offenders may also employ psychologists and counselors.

Colleagues at Work

Correction psychologists and counselors work with a variety of human services staff including program administrators, parole officers, and other specialists such as recreation therapists, teachers, and psychiatrists. The amount of contact with prison guards varies.

Whom Would You Help?

Correction psychologists and counselors work with male or female inmates ranging in age from juveniles to adults of all ages. Prison terms of these inmates may range from a few months to life; some inmates are on "death row" and scheduled for execution.

Correction psychologists accept referrals (inmates) from counselors and others in the prison system. Inmates referred to them may show symptoms of chronic mental illness including schizophrenia and depression. Inmates experiencing situational adjustment difficulties, and alcohol or drug abuse may also be referred to psychologists. All inmates in an institution are on a counselor's caseload.

Job Responsibilities of Psychologists

Job responsibilities of correction psychologists include comprehensive evaluations using a wide variety of psychological procedures and techniques. The psychologist develops and implements a treatment program that may include individual and group therapy. Often the psychologist is asked to perform consultative and advisory duties and may guide others in the application of a therapeutic plan. Supervision of other psychologists and perhaps other human services staff may be expected. It is not uncommon for the psychologist to develop and conduct staff training for institution personnel. A significant responsibility of the correction psychologist is completing paperwork. This documentation might include individual (inmate) contact forms, case disposition forms, psychological reports, and group therapy rosters. The psychologist may also be responsible for some security functions including escorting inmates from one location to another and recording entry and exit from the facility.

Job Responsibilities of Counselors

The correction counselor's responsibilities include a variety of duties using casework and group and individual counseling methods and techniques to help inmates adjust to institutional living. The counselor helps inmates in solving social, economic, and emotional problems with the goal of changing their attitudes and behavior. Counselors also promote the development of a sense of dignity and responsibility. The correction counselor, often called a case manager, is a liaison between the inmate and the rest of the institution and the outside world. The counselor helps the inmate handle day-to-day adjustment problems, grievances, and legal issues.

The correction counselor, often with other staff, develops an individual performance or treatment plan to include such issues as academic or vocational training; employment; and social, economic, and behavioral adjustments. Counselors are responsible for a periodic performance review of the inmates on their caseload. They may also be responsible for classification reviews (change in security level, e.g., from maximum to medium) and parole plans. The correction counselor may experience an excessive amount of paperwork. A conflict is also possible between the role of counselor (e.g., helper) and the role of law enforcement agent (e.g., disciplinarian). The counselor functions within strict security requirements of the institution and, in some instances, must demonstrate proficiency with a firearm at regular intervals.

Personal Characteristics

Correction psychologists and counselors must be able to handle stress and be fair, firm, and consistent. They should be even-tempered, objective, and able to deal with inmates' anger, sarcasm, and other antisocial behavior. Psychologists and counselors must treat each inmate as a unique individual but be careful not to overidentify with an inmate. Awareness of the symptoms of burnout is important.

Correction counselors' entry-level salaries at state institutions range from $19,000 to $24,000. Federal correction counselors often begin employment at the GS-7 level, which has a starting salary of about $19,500.

Education and Training

Correction psychologists have a PhD or PsyD and may or may not be licensed as psychologists by the state. Some states require licensure within a specified time frame. In some states, there are positions in corrections titled Psychological Services Associate, or Clinical Behavioral Specialist. Such positions usually require a master's degree in psychology.

Salary

The starting salary for entry-level correction psychologists with a PhD range from $25,000 to $35,000, depending on the state. Counseling psychologists who work in the federal correction system would begin at the GS-11 level, with a starting salary of approximately $28,800. Correction counselors have a bachelor's degree or a higher degree, but can often substitute related work experience for formal education.

Youth Counselor

In the corrections system, the youth counselor assists in the rehabilitation and social development of delinquent youth. Although youth counselors may be found in most state correctional systems, the entry-level position for this work might be titled Youth Services Worker or Youth Development Aide.

Places to Work

Youth counselors work in juvenile institutions that often focus on academic (high school) preparation. Other youth counselors work in group homes, halfway houses, or outdoor camps.

Colleagues at Work

Youth counselors work closely with youth services workers or aides, if those positions exist in the correctional system. Other colleagues include treatment team coordinators (usually in a supervisory position), case managers, program administrators, and teachers. Relationships may also be established with family members of delinquents, attorneys, psychologists, and community agency staff.

Whom Would You Help?

The age range of juveniles in an institution may be 13 to 19. Typically, the facility is not coeducational. Following conviction for a crime, most juveniles are placed on probation. With subsequent offenses, placement in a juvenile facility is likely. Consequently, most youth in a juvenile institution are multiple offenders for whom probation was not a sufficient punishment to stop them from committing additional offenses.

Job Responsibilities

Usually all facets of the youth's life are supervised by youth counselors including their educational, work, and recreational activities. The youth counselor is responsible for maintaining discipline and socially desirable behavior in accordance with a prescribed treatment or performance plan. The youth counselor may also provide instruction or guidance regarding personal hygiene, nutrition, and dress.

The youth counselor may provide individual and group counseling. The youth counselor works closely with other staff members, families of the juvenile, and staff of other agencies. Periodic and special evaluations (written reports) are necessary. Routine record keeping is also required. Youth counselors are responsible for security; they enforce policies and regulations and help search for and return runaways.

Personal Characteristics

Youth counselors must be patient and exercise good judgment. Maturity is a valuable trait. Because some juveniles exhibit provocative (hostile, abusive, assaultive) behavior, youth counselors must exercise self-control and restraint. The ability to recognize small positive behavior changes and reinforce them is helpful. The youth counselor should also be able to respond quickly and effectively in emergencies.

Education and Training

Depending on the state and the specific job duties, education requirements range from high school graduation to some college coursework.

Salary

The starting salary for youth counselors ranges from $15,000 to $22,000.

Parole Officer

The parole officer performs professional-level work supervising probationers and parolees. In some units of government, probation officer and parole officer are separate occupations. In many government agencies including federal corrections, both functions are performed by the same individual. This description of a parole officer will include probation officer duties.

Places to Work

Parole officers may work for federal, state, county, or municipal agencies. Their office is usually in the community they serve, although some parole officers are employed at correctional institutions.

Colleagues at Work

Parole officers work with other law enforcement personnel including police, attorneys, and judges. They work closely with therapists, teachers, and staff members of a variety of community agencies. The nature of their work also puts them in contact with family members and friends of their clients as well as employers of parolees.

Whom Would You Help?

The parole officer may work with probationers who are individuals adjudicated by a court of law. Because of the nature of the crime or extenuating circumstances, such as a first offense, the individual may be placed on probation or receive a suspended sentence with probation. Parolees are individuals released conditionally from a correctional institution. If they meet the conditions of their parole for the period of time specified, they cease to be under the control of the court system. Probationers and parolees may be male or female and range in age from teenagers to the elderly. Crimes committed by probationers and parolees may range from petty theft to multiple murders.

Job Responsibilities

The overall responsibility of parole officers is to supervise closely the activities of their clients to ensure that they meet the conditions of probation or parole. It is the responsibility of the parole officer to determine what services, including counseling, might be helpful in assisting probationers or parolees. Parole officers assist their clients in their personal, social, and economic adjustment in the community.

The parole officer must perform considerable investigatory work. Such research may be necessary prior to the development of a preparole plan or after a probation or parole violation occurs. Many of the parole officer's activities terminate in paperwork.

Parole officers work closely with employers, educational institutions, and other community agencies that may provide services to their clients such as psychotherapy and alcohol/drug counseling. Parole officers may be required to gather urine samples from some clients for drug screening.

In some governmental units, the parole officer is considered a law enforcement officer and carries a badge and a gun. The parole officer can make arrests when parole violations are indicated and then has the responsibility for prosecuting the individual. A great deal of the parole officer's work is conducted out of the office.

Personal Characteristics

Parole officers must be mature and exercise sound judgment. They should possess integrity, be even-tempered, and have no major problems of their own. The should be able to work independently and be organized and articulate. Parole officers should enjoy challenging work assignments (occasionally dangerous ones), be concerned for their clients but also be aware of the manipulative tactics of some clients.

Education and Training

A bachelor's degree is the usual educational requirement for parole officers although, in some instances, experience can be substituted for some education. In the federal system, probation/parole officers come into the service with at least a bachelor's degree.

Salary

At the state level, starting salaries for parole officers may range from $18,000 to $23,000. Federal probation/parole officers typically begin work at the GS-9 level ($23,800) before moving to the GS-11 level ($28,800).

Vocational Rehabilitation Counselor

Places to Work

State vocational rehabilitation counselors work in a variety of settings. Most work in a state-funded office that may be shared with other state staff from such agencies as social services or employment services. Vocational rehabilitation counselors may be stationed in a state hospital, university campus, Job Service office, or local school district. Others may work at sheltered workshops.

Colleagues at Work

The usual coworkers of a vocational rehabilitation counselor are other counselors, clerical support staff, and supervisory staff. Because of the nature of their work, vocational rehabilitation counselors regularly work with a variety of professionals from several agencies. Some of these professionals are physicians, psychologists, social workers, instructors/trainers, and employment service staff.

Whom Would You Help?

Clients eligible for rehabilitation services have physical or mental limitations. The individuals often have a combination of handicapping conditions with additional problems such as alcohol abuse. Clients range from teenagers to older adults and come from all socioeconomic and ability levels.

Job Responsibilities

The goal of vocational rehabilitation counseling is to assist eligible clients to reach a successful status. Successful closures usually mean employment in a regular job or sheltered workplace. Becoming an independent homemaker or helping in a family business (even without pay) are also successful outcomes.

The vocational rehabilitation counselor is a case manager working with many clients. The counselor proceeds from a comprehensive assessment to the development of a rehabilitation plan appropriate for the client to successful accomplishment of the plan. The counselor arranges for medical, psychological, and vocational examinations and gathers additional data as necessary. In order to assist the client, the vocational rehabilitation counselor can purchase services and materials. For example, prosthetic devices, special equipment, tools, and uniforms may be purchased. Payment for education or training is also possible. The counselor works closely with employers to facilitate job placement. The counselor also consults with employers about job accommodations that may be necessary to employ an individual with handicapping conditions.

The vocational rehabilitation counselor is responsible for the completion of ongoing written narratives, contract forms, letters, and other documents. Most counselors will also visit other agency staff, follow up with service providers, and meet with employers.

Personal Characteristics

Vocational rehabilitation counselors must be able to establish helping relationships with clients who have a wide variety of handicapping conditions. These counselors need strong analytical skills to make use of assessment and evaluation data from multiple sources. They must be able to work with many clients at one time, so organizational skills are critical. Because of the necessary contacts with many resource providers, vocational rehabilitation counselors should have strong oral and written communication skills.

Education and Training

A bachelor's degree and experience in vocational rehabilitation or a master's degree in vocational rehabilitation is required for entry-level positions in state vocational rehabilitation offices. The professional credential in this field is Certified Rehabilitation Counselor (CRC) [see chapter 13].

Salary

Entry-level salaries for state vocational rehabilitation counselors range from $20,000 to $25,000.

Military Counselor

Places to Work

Military counselors work at military bases, naval stations, and military hospitals in the United States and overseas. Small military facilities may not have their own military counselor but could be served by one who travels from place to place. Some military counselor positions remain vacant for long periods of time, and yet one of the potential benefits to the military counselor is international travel.

Colleagues at Work

Military counselors are civilian Department of Defense personnel. Typically, their colleagues at work are also civilian personnel and include clerical assistants, a testing examiner, and a supervisor. In the army and air force, the military counselors' occupational title is Guidance Counselor and their supervisor is an Educational Services Officer. In the navy and marines, the military counselor's official title is Educational Services Specialist. In the marines, some Educational Services Specialists are members of the military, not civilians.

Whom Would You Help?

Military counselors work primarily with active duty military personnel. The majority of counselors' military clients are enlisted personnel, although they also work with officers. Military counselors also help civilians who are employed by the Department of Defense and work at the military facility. Dependents of military personnel are also eligible for services.

The military personnel with whom the counselor works may be relatively new to the service, nearing completion of the required period of enlistment and leaving the service, or retiring from the military with 20 or more years of service. The civilians and dependents with whom the military counselor works have a wide range of ability levels and represent many cultures and countries.

Job Responsibilities

Military counselors are primarily educational counselors. The focus of their work with clients is usually the identification of educational or training opportunities outside the military that will enhance their military career or help prepare them for a postmilitary career. Sometimes career or vocational counseling is necessary before appropriate educational opportunities can be identified.

Enlisted personnel who plan a career in the military are encouraged to complete college-level courses, earn an associate of arts degree or a bachelor's degree in order to enhance promotional possibilities. To help ensure successful careers in the military, officers are encouraged to complete a master's degree.

Military counselors assist their clients in identifying appropriate courses or colleges (sometimes correspondence courses), assist them in applying for admission to college, and help them process tuition assistance requests if appropriate. They also help them evaluate their military training and experience to determine if college credit can be obtained for them. The College Level Examination Program (CLEP) is administered through their office.

Military counselors may also be responsible for other tests administered through the educational service office. Some offices administer the General Educational Development (GED) exam, SAT, ACT, Graduate Record Exam (GRE), and Graduate Management Admissions Test (GMAT).

Other responsibilities of the military counselor include conducting separation briefings for personnel leaving the military. For example, the army has a transition program for 2–3 days addressing such issues as employment-seeking skills, resume writing, educational opportunities, and financial aid. Retirement briefings may also be the responsibility of the military counselor.

In the navy, the counselor may be responsible for assessing military personnel's educational needs and contracting with colleges and other institutions to provide the training following a request for a proposal review process. Other duties of military counselors may include promotion and publicity efforts and education fairs.

Personal Characteristics

Military counselors must have a desire to help people and a concern for their growth and development. Counselors are in a position to expand greatly the educational possibilities of their clients. They do this through their ability to relate to individuals of all cultural and ability levels and their knowledge of educational and other opportunities. Additional personal characteristics desirable for military counselors include patience, dedication, and the ability to stay motivated and knowledgeable of possibilities for their clients.

Training and Education

Although some military counselors may start with less than a master's degree, a master's degree is preferred.

Salary

As civilian employees of the Department of Defense, military counselors are paid in accordance with the General Schedule. The levels for military counselors range from GS-5 to GS-11. With a master's degree, military counselors would usually be at the GS-9 level, which has a starting salary of about $23,000.

Further Information

As indicated earlier, these are just a few of the counseling and human development occupations found in federal and state agencies. Additional information about these and other occupations may be requested directly from such agencies. Information can also be obtained from the *Occupational Outlook Handbook* (OOH) or from the associations named below (addresses may be found in the appendix):

Employment Counselor: National Employment Counselors Association

Correction Counselor/Correction Psychologist: American Psychological Association; Public Offender Counselor Association; American Correctional Association

Youth Counselor: American Correctional Association; Public Offender Counselor Association

Parole Officer: American Correctional Association; Federal Probation Officers Association; Public Offender Counselor Association

Vocational Rehabilitation Counselor: American Rehabilitation Counseling Association; Commission on Rehabilitation Counselor Certification; National Rehabilitation Counseling Association

Military Counselor: American Association for Adult and Continuing Education; Military Educators and Counselors Association

Chapter 10

CAREERS IN HEALTH CARE FACILITIES

Joseph McCormack

Health care facilities for patients with physical problems or emotional difficulties provide a number of employment opportunities for people interested in counseling and human development professions. These facilities offer a variety of positions that demand different levels of training and education. Professionals may work with patients at many stages during the course of treatment.

The array of positions open in health care delivery systems has expanded considerably over the past 20–30 years. First, the health care system has expanded due to increased availability of insured health care. Also, with the holistic health or wellness movement, the number of positions considered part of any health care delivery team has increased to include professions not previously associated with medicine (e.g., health psychology, behavioral medicine, psychotherapy). The future of health care will probably continue to expand as the U.S. population ages and as medical science continues to advance.

There are a number of health care settings in which one might practice. Many private health care settings exist—general hospitals, psychiatric facilities, rehabilitation hospitals, and substance abuse programs. Within the public sector, there are a variety of state and municipal general hospitals and state psychiatric facilities. One of the larger health care employers in the public sector is the Veterans Affairs (VA). The VA has health care facilities in most states and several territories. The VA also has extensive programs of training for a variety of health care professions, including medicine and psychiatry, psychology, social work, nursing, rehabilitation counseling, and occupational therapy.

The following discussion of human services positions in the health care sector will focus both on those professions in health care systems devoted primarily to physical illness and to those dealing with emotional/ psychiatric disorders. The list of professions includes psychologists, health psychologists, mental health counselors, nurses, nursing assistants, psychiatric aides, social workers, occupational and recreational therapists, and rehabilitation counselors.

Psychologist

In mental health care systems, the psychologist functions as a member of a multidisciplinary treatment care delivery team. Generally, such a team consists of psychiatrists, counselors, nurses, nursing assistants, social workers, and other ancillary team members. The psychologist's function and specialty on the team is generally that of psychological testing and consultation regarding diagnosis and treatment planning. The psychologist offers opinions concerning the primary difficulties that patients encounter, and provides suggestions concerning the most appropriate treatment.

It must be added that this is not psychologists' sole responsibility or the only role they can play on a treatment team or in the hospital. With their training in psychotherapy and counseling, psychologists may be responsible for individual, group, or marital/family therapy with patients and their families. In some settings, the psychologist rather than the physician takes the role of team leader, making treatment and administrative decisions concerning patients, and coordinating the functions of the treatment team. Finally, in some cases, psychologists with training in vocational testing and counseling may, in addition to psychological testing, work with patients in vocational planning.

Working as a psychologist requires considerable flexibility as to work settings one can tolerate. The psychologist must be able to work independently, without supervision, yet also possess the capacity to work both with other professionals and with patients. While being self-directed and self-initiating, psychologists must also be flexible enough to receive input from other team members and coordinate their efforts with the overall effort of the treatment team. In their role as therapists, psychologists must have a capacity for empathy and for tolerance of individuals with divergent life-styles who may at times behave in an idiosyncratic, sometimes unpleasant manner.

In health care settings, the psychologist generally has an advanced (master's or doctoral) degree in counseling, clinical psychology, or counseling psychology. Training as a psychologist or counselor can take place at either the master's or the doctoral level. Most states require a PhD (Doctor of Philosophy) or PsyD (Doctor of Psychology) degree for the psychologist to be licensed.

The PhD degree requires generally between 4 and 6 years of graduate school beyond the bachelor's degree. Coursework is focused on both the core academic requirements in psychology (learning theory, physiological psychology, and social psychology) and in a specialty (clinical or counseling), which may include coursework in assessment, psychotherapy and counseling, vocational assessment and counseling, and psychopathology. The PhD degree generally requires completion of a dissertation based on empirical research. The PsyD degree, although not always requiring a research dissertation, generally requires completion of a major independent project.

The master's degree in psychology requires 1 to 3 years of post-bachelor's study. The coursework is similar to that required for the PhD but is generally not as extensive. Many master's programs require completion of a research-based master's thesis.

The master's degree is also offered in counseling. Usually a master's degree in counseling is offered through a school of education rather than through a psychology department. Coursework for a master's degree in counseling varies, with some programs requiring virtually the same coursework as for a master's degree in psychology, and others requiring more coursework in education, counseling, and therapy. It may be possible to obtain a license at the master's level in counseling or psychology, but this varies from state to state. In over 30 states, however, licensure as a counselor has been adopted, and a person with a counseling master's degree may obtain licensure this way (see chapter 13).

The *Occupational Outlook Handbook* (U.S. Department of Labor, 1988) [called the OOH] lists the average salary for psychologists with a PhD as $39,500 in hospitals and clinics. Salary for psychologists in other nonprofit agencies averages $32,400; for those in state government agencies, hospitals, and clinics the salary is $32,900. For master's level psychologists and counselors with one year's experience, the average salary is listed as $22,500. The System of Interactive Guidance and Information [called SIGI] (Educational Testing Service, 1988) reports the average beginning salary of PhD psychologists as between $24,000 to $31,000 per year. The median income of all psychologists is reported to be approximately $36,000 for counseling psychologists and $44,000 for clinical psychologists.

Health Psychologist

A new area of specialization for clinical and counseling psychology is the field of health psychology. With the growing awareness that medical difficulties and illnesses have an emotional component and that there is a relationship between body and mind, health psychology has asserted itself as a discipline that has a contribution to make in the treatment of medical illness. Health psychology as a professional discipline has a variety of names, including health psychology, behavioral medicine, holistic health or medicine, and psychosomatic medicine.

The health psychologist fulfills a number of roles in the health care establishment. One role is that of consultant to the medical treatment team, consisting of physicians, nurses, nursing assistants, and social workers. The psychologist consults about psychological factors that might affect the course of an illness, either for better or worse—patient morale, medication compliance, and family dynamics that can foster or impede recovery. With some patients whose problems may be multifaceted or where it is difficult to determine the degree of emotional versus physical involvement in the etiology or maintenance of illness, the psychologist may be called upon to utilize psychological testing to make a differential diagnosis.

One of the results of the increasing effectiveness of medicine in treating infectious disease has been the growing realization that the patient can control factors that prevent disease or contribute to cure. Factors such as smoking, diet, and exercise have received increasing attention as areas in which the patient's habits may determine whether disease occurs or is prevented, especially with conditions such as heart disease, lung cancer, emphysema, and stroke. Growing out of this awareness, the health psychologist has been called upon to develop techniques to promote healthy habits and alter unhealthy habits. Such techniques, referred to as habit management, are performed individually or in groups and include issues such as smoking cessation, diet management, stress management, and medication compliance. In addition, given the role stress has been found to play in physical and psychological illnesses, the health psychologist may be called upon to perform techniques such as biofeedback and relaxation training, both for patients and staff. With patients who are terminally ill, the health psychologist may work with both the patient and the patient's family, helping them to deal with grief and loss issues.

Functioning as a health psychologist requires virtually all of the characteristics described above in our discussion of the psychologist, namely self-reliance plus the ability to work with other professionals, and empathy and tolerance of diverse client life-styles. In addition, work as a health psychologist requires that the person be able to work with physically ill persons and medical teams.

Licensure and training for health psychologists is virtually the same as for psychologists working in psychiatric settings. The health psychologist area is, in large part, a specialty with the field of clinical or counseling psychology, or counseling. The starting salaries reported for psychologists in psychiatric settings are similar for health psychologists.

Counselor

Counselors work in a variety of capacities within the health care delivery system. Because counselor training can cover a wide area, counselors, depending on their training, may be able to apply their skills in such diverse fields as individual and group psychotherapy, psychological testing, marital or family therapy, vocational testing or counseling, alcohol or drug dependence counseling, rehabilitation services, health psychology, behavioral medicine, and behavior therapy or management. In these various settings the counselor may be part of a treatment team, or may be part of an independent department to whom the hospital treatment team refers patients.

Personal qualities those who wish to be counselors need include the ability to work independently and to take initiative. Also important is a tolerance for ambiguity and for varying client life-styles. A curiosity about human behavior and a willingness to explore painful issues with clients and within oneself are also helpful qualities.

Counselor training can be obtained at the bachelor's, master's, and doctoral levels. The degree program offered varies among universities. Some typical programs include counseling, counselor education, counseling psychology, counseling and personnel services, and educational counseling. At the bachelor's and master's level, coursework and a practicum or internship is generally required; an independent research thesis is sometimes required. At the doctoral level, coursework, a year-long internship, and a doctoral research dissertation is almost always required.

Licensure for counselors has become more prevalent among the states. For licensure, most states require a master's degree from an accredited university, and postgraduate experience. Many states also require that applicants pass a licensure exam. for those trained in psychology programs, especially at the doctoral level, licensure as a psychologist may be possible. Starting salary for counselors varies with the duties one performs and the setting in which one works.

Therapists Using Artistic Media

Music, art, and dance therapists work with people in both physical medicine and mental health facilities. These professionals utilize artistic media—music, art, dance, and drama—to achieve nonartistic goals with patients. For example, a dance therapist might use involvement in dance therapy to change the nonverbal behavior of a depressed patient whose posture droops and whose gait is slowed. Music therapists may use recorded music and work with patients playing instruments to help patients relax, increase their socialization skills, enhance physical dexterity in those who have physical mobility problems, and enhance capacities for attention and concentration. These therapists work with patients with all types of difficulties—mentally retarded patients, psychiatric patients, those recovering from physical injuries and strokes, and those needing relaxation skills.

A hospital treatment team often refers patients for help to the music, art, or dance therapist. The therapist assesses the patient's physical or emotional needs and goals and attempts to develop activities to address those needs and goals. These therapists' observations of the patient can be especially useful to the team because they see the patient in a different setting.

Personal qualities people who go into these professions need include an interest in working with and helping people, patience, and flexibility and creativity in finding ways to engage patients in tasks.

Training in dance, music, and art therapy varies with the discipline. For those going into music therapy, training can be obtained at the bachelor's, master's, and doctoral levels. For those in art therapy, training can be obtained at the master's and doctoral levels. The same is true of dance therapy. To get into master's or doctoral programs in these fields you should have had some background in art or dance during your undergraduate training. The primary degree for music therapists is either the bachelor's or master's degree; for art and dance therapy, the primary degree is a master's degree.

Certification and registration vary with each discipline. Music therapists are certified by the National Certification Board for Music Therapy. Passing of an examination is required for certification. The National Association for Music Therapy offers the title Registered Music Therapist (RMT) and the American Association for Music Therapy offers certification as a Certified Music Therapist (CMT). The certifications require a bachelor's degree plus internship, but no examination. Dance therapists are nationally certified by the American Dance Therapy Association. A master's degree in dance therapy is required. For art therapists, certification is through the American Art Therapy Association and requires a master's degree in art therapy; no examination is currently given. Settings vary as to whether practitioners require certification in one of these specialties. Although some settings do not require certification, the number of settings requiring it continues to grow.

At the Veterans Affairs, the starting salary for a music therapist with a bachelor's degree is approximately $15,700. For those with a master's degree, the average starting salary is $17,500. Starting salaries vary in other settings.

Psychology Technician

In some health care settings, individuals with bachelor's or master's level training in psychology work as psychology technicians. The psychology technician or psychology aide, as the occupation is sometimes termed, works under the supervision of a PhD level psychologist. The duties of the psychology technician vary from setting to setting. In some work settings psychology technicians function much like psychologists, conducting therapy and structured groups under the psychologist's supervision. In other settings, the psychology technician's responsibilities are more administrative; in these settings the technician may administer and score psychological testing for the psychologist, who then interprets the tests and writes the test report. In either case, the psychology technician has direct patient contact, either as a therapist or as a test administrator. The psychology technician may be part of the multidisciplinary treatment team, sharing observations of the patient. In medical health care settings, the technician may either lead or assist the psychologist in leading management groups, may consult with the team about patients' problems, or administer psychological tests.

Personal characteristics necessary for the occupation of psychology technician include empathy and the ability to work with either physically or mentally ill patients. Dependability is important, as well as the ability to work under supervision and to carry out treatment plans with patients.

Training as a psychology technician generally requires a bachelor's degree in psychology or a related field (sociology, social work, counseling). For some technician positions a master's degree in psychology or counseling is necessary. Once on the job, the technician may be trained further in the specific tests to administer, or the therapeutic procedures to use. Currently, there is no licensure or certification for psychology technicians, although some states have licensure for master's-level psychologists, or for licensed mental health technicians.

The average salary for entry-level psychology technicians with a bachelor's degree within the federal system is $14,800, according to the OOH; for a master's level individual with one year's experience, the average salary is $22,500.

Social Worker

In health care settings, social workers play a variety of roles and fulfill numerous responsibilities. In psychiatric settings, social workers function as part of the multidisciplinary treatment team. Often the social worker serves as liaison with the patient's family and as liaison between the patient, the hospital, and the community in planning the circumstances to which the patient will be discharged. Additionally, the social worker in a psychiatric setting conducts a social history assessment that details the patient's family, social, occupational, and marital functioning throughout the patient's life span. The social assessment can be particularly helpful in conceptualizing and understanding the patient's difficulties. Social workers in psychiatric settings also have responsibility for psychotherapy. As do psychiatrists, psychologists, counselors, and some nurses, social workers generally have training in psychotherapy and counseling with individuals, families, and groups.

In some settings social workers have administrative responsibilities. Social workers may function as health care unit directors, supervising the activities of other professionals. They also may function as clinical team leaders, making decisions concerning treatment disposition for patients.

In physical health care settings, like in psychiatric settings, social workers make a major contribution by being a liaison with the family and the community. Specifically, social workers are often responsible for discharge planning, ensuring that the settings to which patients are discharged will facilitate recovery. The social worker may be instrumental in facilitating an optimal return to the occupational world at the appropriate level. For those patients needing extra family, community, or professional support, the social worker is often the person on the team who makes the necessary arrangements with the family, community agencies, or relevant support groups (e.g., diabetic support groups, medication maintenance groups) to provide that support. Another function the social worker often provides is the assessment of psychological factors involved in the patient's illness/recovery (e.g., medication compliance, depression secondary to disability, anxiety concerning medical procedures or recovery).

Social work as a profession in general requires a number of personal characteristics. Personal flexibility and the capacity to tolerate and work with people of different cultures, values, and life-styles is significant. The ability to work both independently and with people is important. Communication skills are of value, as is the capacity to know and work with systems and bureaucracies, facilitating client usage of the system.

Training in social work takes place at both the bachelor's and the master's level. In most health settings, the degree required for professional practice is the master's degree (MSW), although in some settings a bachelor's degree (BSW) is allowed. The Committee on Social Work Education (CSWE) accredits both BSW and MSW programs in social work.

Social work licensure has grown as more and more states pass licensure laws sanctioning the profession of social work. Some states require an MSW, whereas other states license both BSW and MSW social workers. Some states have a two- or three-tier system of licensure, with one level for bachelor's-level social workers, a second for master's-level workers, and a third for master's-level social workers who are clinical specialists in a given area.

The average beginning salary for social workers is between $14,000 and $21,000, depending on the setting and education (Educational Testing Service, 1988). Those social workers with a master's degree or a higher degree can expect to earn more. The *Occupational Outlook Handbook* (OOH) lists the average starting salary for BSW-level social workers as about $16,000 to $17,000. For those with the MSW the average starting salary is listed as between $20,000 and $22,000.

Nurse

In both the medical and psychiatric settings, nurses play a central role. The role of nursing personnel in health care settings is expanding in the scope of responsibilities performed.

In psychiatric settings, nursing personnel have a variety of responsibilities. Nurses are responsible for observing patients' behavior, and reporting their observations to the staff. The observations they are responsible for range from patient behavior and social interaction, to more traditional medical observations such as blood pressure, temperature, and other vital signs. Although the physician is responsible for writing orders and directing treatment on a psychiatric unit, nursing staff are, in general, responsible for implementing the treatment plan on the ward. Nurses are responsible for the smooth functioning of the ward; they implement ward policies, set appropriate limits on patients' maladaptive behaviors, dispense prescribed medications, and are responsible for crisis management and therapeutic listening to patients' concerns. This latter, informal counseling may be the only therapeutic conversation the patient receives in some hospital settings. For those nurses who have received training in counseling and psychotherapy, formal therapy may be part of their job duties.

In physical medicine settings, the nurse is responsible for implementing of the patients's treatment plan. The nurse dispenses medications and preforms procedures ordered by the physician. The nurse is responsible for making both routine observations of patient vital signs, and whatever other monitoring of patient functioning is requested by the physician or the team. Interpersonally, the nurse is the staff member who has the greatest amount of contact with the patient; often it is the nurse's ability to empathize with the patient's fears, anxieties, and hopes that contributes the most to the patient's morale. Similarly, given that the physician is often absent, it is the nurse who must convey vital information about the patient to the patient's relatives.

As can be seen from the above discussion, the nurse's role in both physical and mental health settings is central, and often the nurse is the professional with whom the patient has the greatest amount of contact, along with nursing assistants. Such a central role requires special personal characteristics and interpersonal competencies. The nurse must, for instance, be able to be both an empathic listener and an effective limit setter. In working with disturbed patients, the limit-setting role often requires that the nurse be able to tolerate patient anger without retaliating, as well as being able to set limits and enlist the patient's compliance. Sharp observational skills are called for, as well as the ability to communicate these observations effectively to other staff on the team. Also, the ability to take initiative on one's own in a crisis is important, as is the ability to work effectively as a team member and to implement the team's and the physician's decisions and recommendations. The ability to be a liaison with family is important as well. In physical medical settings, tolerance for the results of surgical procedures is required.

Training for the nursing profession can take place at several levels. Training for the registered nurse (RN) degree can be obtained either through a 4-year university program leading to the bachelor of science in nursing (BSN), or through a hospital-based nurses' training program (RN). At the master's and PhD levels, nurse practitioner training is available in specialties such as mental health, pediatrics, family practice, women's health, midwifery, and other areas. Both coursework and practical experience under supervision are required. For the licensed practical nurse (LPN) degree, training in a 2-year associate degree program is required. This can take place at a community college or vocational-technical school. Programs at both the bachelor's and associate's level are accredited by the National League of Nursing; also, most states have a Board of Nursing that is responsible for accrediting programs within their state.

In 1985, the American Nurses' Association voted to support the bachelor's degree in nursing as the professional nursing degree, with the associate of arts degree being considered preparatory for technical nursing practice. Although this is not the recognized standard everywhere, it is well on its way to becoming the established standard (American Nurses' Association, 1988).

Licensing as an RN or a technical nurse is conducted by state licensing bodies. All states have licensing for RNs and LPNs. Consult your state's board of nursing for specifics of licensure.

The average starting salary for LPNs is $14,700 according to the OOH. The average starting salary for RNs with a bachelor's degree is $20,400. SIGI (ETS, 1988) lists the average starting salary for RNs as between $18,000 and $24,000. The median income for RNs is approximately $28,000. For LPNs the average starting salary is $12,000 to $15,000, with the median income nationwide being $17,500.

Nurse's Aide/Psychiatric Aide

The nursing assistant or psychiatric aide often has the greatest amount of direct contact with the patient. Thus, this occupation is central to the health care delivery system. Nursing assistants work with the supervision of a registered nurse or licensed practical nurse. Their duties include helping patients with self-care, feeding, dressing, and bathing when they are unable to do so for themselves; monitoring patient physical complaints and reporting these to the nurse or physician; and escorting patients to appointments or activities. In psychiatric settings, psychiatric aides often spend a great deal of time socializing with and participating in recreation with patients. With the nurse, the nurse's aide or psychiatric aide is often the one most responsible for implementing the team treatment plan in a practical "nuts-and-bolts" way. In addition the aide may participate in implementing ward structure, setting limits, helping delusional patients become more reality-oriented, and intervening in crises under nursing supervision. With assaultive or otherwise out-of-control patients, the aide is responsible for getting the patient into a seclusion room or restraining the patient.

Characteristics important for a nurse's aide or psychiatric aide include responsibility, caring for people, and a tolerance for provocative behavior. Also necessary is the ability to work with team members, to communicate well, and to set limits on inappropriate behavior.

Psychiatric aide and nursing assistant positions usually require no special training to begin with. A high school diploma may not be required. Most hospitals have orientation programs where the assistant learns basic patient care skills—how to monitor vital signs such as temperature and blood pressure, how to lift patients who cannot move on their own, and bathing patients. In psychiatric settings, the aide is trained in interpersonal skills, communication techniques, socialization interventions, and effective listening skills.

The OOH reports the median average income for nursing assistants and psychiatric aides to be $10,700.

Rehabilitation Counselor

In both physical and psychiatric health care settings, clients and patients may suffer from varying degrees of impairment that may affect social and occupational functioning. Often the patients must, as a result of their illness, adjust to the task of finding a different occupation or to the reality that they are no longer employable. Rehabilitation counselors are responsible for working with patients, assessing the degree of their limitations, and helping them to adjust to those limitations occupationally.

The rehabilitation counselor works with the treatment team, which may have been the source of the initial referral of the patient for rehabilitation. The rehabilitation counselor assesses the patient's level of disability, using medical, social, psychiatric, testing, and nursing information, and may also administer a variety of vocational interest and ability tests to gain a better understanding of the client's impairment. Once an assessment is made of the patient's level of disability, the counselor works with the client to develop a plan for rehabilitation. Vocational plans may include training for a new job, continued education, or recommendation of occupations the client might pursue. Vocational rehabilitation plans are often behavioral in nature and require the counselor to exercise skills in planning and to specify steps to be taken by the client and requirements to be made of the client. The counselor also identifies potential obstacles to the completion of the plan. The counselor is responsible for foreseeing obstacles, and in those instances where help can be obtained to overcome those obstacles, referring the client to resources that may be of assistance. Additionally, the counselor may assist the patient with occupational placement. These tasks require coordination both with the patient's treatment team as well as with the community at large when considering training and placement. Another difficult task that falls to the rehabilitation counselor is determining the client's eligibility for rehabilitation funds, as well as the client's potential for succeeding in rehabilitation programs, a task that may often involve refusing a client something the client wishes.

Personal qualities necessary for the occupation of rehabilitation counselor include the ability to work both with patients and other professionals. Knowledge of community agencies, businesses, and public bureaucracies—that may be sources of employment for clients—is necessary. The rehabilitation counselor also should possess a capacity to understand the experience of the client, along with the ability to make specific plans and the ability to assess what the client can handle. With shrinking budgets, and the responsibility to determine who can and who cannot benefit from training and other rehabilitation programs, the ability to set realistic limits on client expectations is an increasingly important personal qualification.

Training in rehabilitation counseling can take place at either the master's or the doctoral level. At the master's level, there are approximately 80 programs in rehabilitation counseling. Thirty-three institutions offer the doctoral degree. The Council on Rehabilitation Education (CORE) [see chapter 13] is responsible for accrediting rehabilitation programs. SIGI (ETS, 1988) lists average starting salaries for master's-level rehabilitation counselors as $17,000 to $23,000. Rehabilitation counselors' median salary is reported as $26,000 to $34,000 per year. Salaries vary with education and experience (see chapter 11 also).

Occupational Therapist

Often the recovery of the patient depends on the degree to which the patient can resume normal activities or cope with the limitations their illness has induced. Occupational therapists help patients move toward the goal of resuming normal activities.

Occupational therapists work both in medical health care settings and in psychiatric settings. In medical settings, the occupational therapist's task is to work with the patient, developing activities the patient can utilize to work toward rehabilitation. For example, the occupational therapist working with a stroke victim might design activities or provide instruments with which the patient can work to regain fine motor control. Occupational therapists are concerned with helping patients regain skills of daily living. Due to loss of function, the client may be unable to dress, groom, or bathe, and the occupational therapist's task is to find alternative ways in which the client can accomplish these tasks independently.

In mental health settings, the occupational therapist uses structured activities such as woodworking, leather work, ceramics, or horticulture to promote the patient's socialization and rehabilitation. In these tasks, the occupational therapist contributes to the patient's treatment by helping the patient to learn or relearn such psychological functions as impulse control, planning, delay of gratification, and working with other people cooperatively.

In both medical and mental health settings, occupational therapists are often members of the treatment team. Their observations of the patient are especially of value because occupational therapists see patients in a setting different than the hospital ward, and thus see different patient behavior than the other staff.

Personal characteristics necessary for the job of occupational therapist include the capacity to work with people who are ill, either physically or mentally. The ability to tolerate patient anger and frustration when they are unable to do a task is also necessary. Along with the ability to tolerate patients' feelings, however, the occupational therapist must have the ability to confront inappropriate behavior and to direct the patient toward more appropriate behavior. The capacity to find creative ways to accomplish this sort of direction is helpful. In addition to the ability to work with patients, the occupational therapist needs the capacity to work with team members and to communicate observations to the team effectively.

Training to become an occupational therapist requires a bachelor's degree in occupational therapy. Regulation of the occupational therapy profession is the case in 25 states and provinces. These states have either licensure or trademark laws. A degree in occupational therapy is required to be licensed. Also national certification is possible through the American Occupational Therapy Certification Board (AOTCB), which confers the title of Registered Occupational Therapist (ROT) [see chapter 13].

The average starting salary for occupational therapists with a bachelor's degree is approximately $21,000, according to the OOH. Occupational therapists with experience may earn an average of $26,000. SIGI lists starting salaries for occupational therapists as between $19,000 and $24,000, with median income for occupational therapists being between $26,000 and $29,000.

Recreation Therapist

The recreation therapist utilizes recreational or leisure activities to assist in the patient's physical or emotional recovery from illness. With those suffering from physical illness, the recreation therapist uses activities to assist in regaining lost functions, developing new living skills to adapt to lost capacities, improving morale and helping patients temporarily take their minds off difficulties, managing stress, and building self-confidence and independence. In mental health care facilities, the recreational therapist uses leisure activities to bring patients out of self-imposed isolation or depressive states; to teach socialization skills; to enhance cognitive abilities such as thinking clearly, planning, and controlling impulses; and to teach nonharmful leisure activities. The recreational therapist interviews and assesses patients' values, attitudes, and feelings about leisure and recreation, as well as the patient's physical or emotional needs. On the basis of this assessment, the therapist determines a recreational plan, gearing recreational activities to the patient's values and attitudes as well as to the patient's health care needs. Recreational therapists, like most other health care professionals discussed in this chapter, are often on a treatment team, where they give feedback concerning observations of the patient.

Personal characteristics helpful to the recreation therapist include the ability to work with people. Skill in creatively engaging difficult or uncooperative patients in activities is needed, as is the ability to teach and direct patient activities.

Training to become a recreational therapist requires a bachelor's degree in recreation or leisure. Recreational therapists have a national certification system through the National Therapeutic Recreation Society (NTRS), a division of the National Parks and Recreation Association. The title one earns with certification is Certified Therapeutic Recreation Specialist (CTRS) [see chapter 13]. Certification requires a bachelor's degree plus an internship under the supervision of a CTRS. Although certification is not required for employment as a recreation therapist, it is becoming desirable in a growing number of hospitals and health care centers.

The average starting salary of occupational therapists is $21,000–$25,000.

Summary

A number of helping occupations in the health care field have been reviewed. Those discussed in this chapter represent only some of the occupations available. Careers in medicine as a physician or physician's assistant, various medical technology occupations (e.g., radiology technician), and physical therapy are among the occupations that have not been discussed. For more in-depth treatment of these occupations and the ones discussed in this chapter, the *Occupational Outlook Handbook* (OOH) is a good beginning source.

Further Information

For further information, school counselors and college counseling centers have more occupational information. Information can be obtained from professional associations about many of the occupations described in this chapter. Their addresses can be found in the appendix.

Counselors and Mental Health Counselors: American Association for Counseling and Development; American Mental Health Counselors Association
Dance Therapists: American Dance Therapy Association; National Association for Dance Therapy

Music Therapists: American Association for Music Therapy; National Association for Music Therapy
Nursing: American Nurses' Association
Occupational Therapists: American Occupational Therapy Association
Psychologists and Health Psychologists: American Psychological Association
Recreation Therapists: American Therapeutic Recreation Association; National Council on Therapeutic Recreation; National Parks and Recreation Association
Rehabilitiation Counselors: American Rehabilitation Counseling Association; National Rehabilitation Counseling Association
Social Workers: National Association for Social Work
Therapists Using Artistic Media: National Association for Poetry Therapy; American Art Therapy Association, Inc.

References

American Nurses' Association. (1988). *Nursing Education: Enrolling in a college or university*. Available from American Nurses' Association, 2420 Pershing Road, Kansas City, MO 64108.

Educational Testing Service. (1988). *SIGI: System of Interactive Guidance and Information* (Computer Program). Princeton, NJ: Educational Testing Service.

U.S. Department of Labor. (1988). *Occupational outlook handbook*. Scottsdale, AZ: Associated Book Publishers.

Chapter 11

CAREERS IN RESIDENTIAL TREATMENT CENTERS

Ross K. Lynch and Susan M. Wiegmann

A *rehabilitation facility* is a place where individuals with disabilities overcome or adjust to their functional limitations. Rehabilitation facilities have the following features: (a) a protected environment where individuals can obtain skills, support, and supervision fundamental to their overall development without some of the distractions and tensions of outside society, (b) a team approach by specialists who coordinate individual services and areas of expertise to meet clients' needs as they progress toward their rehabilitation goals, and (c) a program goal of helping individuals move from a dependent to an independent role (Wright, 1980). A *residential treatment facility* is a rehabilitation facility where individuals live for the duration of their treatment.

Many client populations are served in residential treatment facilities (e.g., the mentally ill, developmentally disabled); however, in addition to such traditional patient/client populations, recent years have witnessed a significant increase in the number of persons who have suffered catastrophic injuries. For example, people with severe head injuries are surviving their injuries more frequently than in the past and, as a result, there has been an increase in the number of rehabilitation programs serving such individuals. In these situations, a residential treatment center is a step between inpatient treatment and independent living. This chapter will describe services and occupations found in various residential treatment facilities.

Transitional living centers are residential programs in the community. These programs are also called community reentry programs. They are designed for medically stable individuals with good potential for living independently but whose behavioral or cognitive problems are not well managed in the home community or on an outpatient basis. The focus of

121

a community reentry program is to provide persons with the necessary skills to live as independently and productively as possible within their home community. Clients are admitted (a) from acute care settings where recovery has been rapid but not complete, so that the individual is beyond the need for an acute rehabilitation unit, but not ready to return to the community; (b) from acute rehabilitation settings where the individual has progressed in treatment but needs therapy to develop skills necessary to reenter the community; and (c) from the community when rehabilitation and development of community reentry skills have not been accomplished and the individual has continued to have problems. Duration of stay at the transitional treatment center can be from 3 months to 2 years.

Residents in treatment facilities receive daily therapies provided by an interdisciplinary team. A treatment team is typically composed of a physical therapist, occupational therapist, speech pathologist, psychologist, vocational rehabilitation counselor, registered nurse, family specialist, behavior specialist, and cognitive specialist (McMahon, Shaw, & Maheffey, 1988). In an interdisciplinary model, team members work together on the assessment and definition of outcome goals and a treatment plan. During the treatment phase, team members work independently and are responsible for objectives specific to their occupational specialty. The treatment team conducts an integrated evaluation and synthesizes assessment information from each discipline into a single report. The report provides an overall picture of client functioning and frames realistic outcome goals and objectives toward which all team members can contribute while serving the client (Leland, Lewis, Hinman, & Carrillo, 1988).

Successful reintegration of patients into the community requires many professionals working together to help individuals function well. The roles and functions of these various professionals in the residential treatment program are as follows.

Physical Therapist

Physical therapists carry out a physical restoration program to help alleviate disability and pain. These therapists evaluate the individual disabled by illness or accident to determine the extent of functional limitation and plan a therapeutic program in consultation with the individual's physician. The program may consist of exercises to develop strength, muscle reeducation, and increased range of motion. Physical therapy is often provided to improve and maintain the disabled individual's motor functions. Physical therapists focus on activities such as improving balance, muscle strength, and voluntary control, leading to improved ambulation and physical movements. Physical therapists usually have a bachelor's or master's degree in physical therapy, and physical therapists in most states must be licensed. The national salary range for beginning physical therapists is $21,600 to $25,700 per year. Experienced therapists earn $4,000 to $7,000 more per year.

Occupational Therapist

The primary purpose of occupational therapy is to help people achieve or maintain their capacities to function in daily living activities. Occupational therapy includes self-care activities (eating, dressing, personal hygiene, grooming, handling objects), work activities (related to school, home management, and employment), and recreation or leisure (games, sports, hobbies, and social activities). Occupational therapists usually have bachelor's degrees and earn entry salaries of $21,000 to $25,000 per year. Experienced therapists average $3,000 to $5,000 more per year.

Speech-Language Therapist

Speech-language pathologists work with people who have speech and language problems. They perform tests to find the kind of speech problem a person has, and develop a therapy program to help the person speak more effectively. In addition to working directly with the individual, speech therapists also work with the family because carryover of the learning on a day-to-day basis is essential. Most rehabilitation facilities require a master's degree in speech-language pathology. An additional requirement may be that the speech-language pathologist have earned a Certificate of Clinical Competence from the American Speech, Language, and Hearing Association (ASHA). In order to become certified, it is necessary to have a master's degree and 9 months of professional work under the supervision of a certified speech-language pathologist. Candidates must then pass a national exam. The national salary range is $21,000 to $30,000.

Psychologist

Psychologists study human behavior and mental processes to understand, explain, or help people change their behavior. Psychologists must have a doctoral degree in psychology to qualify for clinical and counseling positions. A large number of psychologists working in rehabilitation settings have completed educational programs in psychology emphasizing clinical, counseling, developmental psychology, neuropsychology, or rehabilitation psychology. The psychologist's knowledge and training is integrated and applied in areas such as neuropsychology, cognitive rehabilitation, behavior management, and individual and group psychotherapy. The psychologist must have well-developed assessment and diagnostic skills, along with a working knowledge of various intervention strategies (Barry & O'Leary, 1989). For example, proficiency in behavior management, neuropsychology, or family therapy is often an important qualification (McMahon et al., 1988). Individuals with doctoral degrees in psychology working in private practice generally have higher earnings than other psychologists. Starting salaries average from $20,000 to over $40,000 per year.

An area of specialization within the field of psychology that is important when working with individuals with head injury is neuropsychology. Neuropsychology is the study of the relationship between the brain and behavior. The neuropsychologist is responsible for the evaluation and treatment of individuals, specifically the behavioral changes that occur when people receive brain injuries. They also determine what method of treatment can be used to improve behavior after an injury (Golden, 1988). Cognitive functions such as intelligence, verbal comprehension, verbal reasoning, memory and learning, visual/spatial abilities, and problem solving are addressed. Additionally, tactile, auditory, and visual perception as well as motor abilities (e.g., eye-hand coordination) are assessed. Neuropsychologists also determine emotional functioning (e.g., reaction to impaired abilities) as well as depression or anxiety that may interfere with cognitive functions (Hallauerm, Prosser, & Swift, 1989) and overall rehabilitation outcome. Neuropsychologists are certified by the American Board of Clinical Neuropsychology after receiving a dotorate in psychology and 5 years' experience in the field. Neuropsychologists may also need to be licensed by the state in which they practice.

Recreation Therapist

Therapeutic recreation is a specialized field within the recreation profession. The recreational therapist plans and directs recreational activities for individuals recovering from physical and mental illness or coping with disability. Activities are planned based on the needs and limitations of the individual. Recreational activities help develop social networks that have been identified as a key variable in the outcome of rehabilitation. A degree in therapeutic recreation (or in recreation with an emphasis on therapeutic recreation) is the usual requirement for clinical positions in this field.

Rehabilitation Counselor

Rehabilitation counselors work with individuals with physical, mental, or emotional disabilities to help them adjust to their disability. Rehabilitation counselors provide counseling services as well as other services, depending on the particular employment setting. Treatment programs that specialize in vocational rehabilitation generally require rehabilitation counselors to have a master's degree in rehabilitation counseling, counseling and guidance, or counseling psychology. Usually, 2 years of study, including a period of supervised clinical experience, are required for the master's degree. Some employers may accept applicants with a bachelor's degree in rehabilitation services, counseling, psychology, or related fields. In addition to educational preparation, certification may be necessary to qualify for particular positions. To become certified, counselors must meet educational and experiential standards established by the Commission on Rehabilitation Counselor Certification and pass a written examination.

Vocational Rehabilitation Counselor

In residential treatment facilities vocational rehabilitation counseling positions vary depending on the level of education of the service provider. Individuals with bachelor's degrees in rehabilitation services or entry-level graduate training are often employed as life skills counselors. The life skills counselor is a primary provider of instructional services for clients to facilitate their movement toward individually determined behavioral self-management, independent living, or vocational goals. These professionals primarily provide community reentry services and are involved in such duties as job coaching, implementation of behavioral plans, and active instruction in daily living skills. Rehabilitation counselors with master's degrees and appropriate experience are more likely to be employed as behavioral specialists, personal adjustment counselors, vocational specialists, or case managers.

Behavioral Specialist

The behavioral specialist directs and supports the behavioral emphasis of the program across all aspects of program activities and services. Behavioral specialists also design, implement, and train staff to implement programs that increase the client's appropriate social behavior.

Personal Adjustment Counselor

The personal adjustment counselor works closely with the psychosocial adjustment issues of the client and family to clarify goals and expectations, provide counseling and support, and advocate for the client and family when needed. The primary responsibility of the personal adjustment counselor is the maximum development of personal, environmental, and interpersonal growth of the clients and their reintegration into the community. The vocational specialist provides vocational evaluation, counseling, training, job coaching, placement, and follow-up services to assist clients in attaining their maximum level of vocational functioning. Salaries generally range from $15,000 to $30,000 per year, and counselors with master's degrees earn more than those with bachelor's degrees.

Case Manager

Case management refers to the managerial activities that facilitate the movement of each client through the service process. Case managers are leaders of the rehabilitation team. They develop treatment plans based on the written assessments of team members. Case managers are coordinators of medical, psychosocial, vocational, educational, cognitive, communication, and recreational services. In this role, the case manager performs functions involving the design, monitoring, and evaluation of individually designed treatment plans; client advocacy; liaison to the family and to the funding sources; and staff supervision. Rehabilitation counselors are often hired for these positions, although individuals from other helping professions may also be employed in this capacity.

Registered Nurse

In a residential treatment facility, registered nurses (RNs) observe, assess, and record physical symptoms, reactions, and progress. They also administer medication, assist in rehabilitation, instruct individuals and their families in proper health care, and help individuals and groups take steps to improve or maintain health and wellness. There are three ways to become a registered nurse. One is obtaining a bachelor's degree in nursing. It is also possible to graduate from a vocational school with a 2-year degree. A few hospitals have nursing school programs that usually involve 3 years of classroom and clinical instruction. Salaries for RNs generally range from $22,700 to $30,900 per year (see chapter 10).

Social Worker

Family specialists or social workers help individuals, families, and groups to cope with various problems through direct counseling or referral to other services. Family members need to be educated about the consequences of disabilities and possible short- and long-term problems that may arise. The social worker is the liaison between the family and the rehabilitation team and is primarily responsible for facilitating family involvement. The social worker may be responsible for discharge planning—helping with all the necessary arrangements to leave a residential facility. A master's degree in social work is preferred for most clinical positions in residential treatment facilities. Two years of specialized study, including 900 hours of supervised field instruction or internship, are required to earn a master's degree in social work. With a bachelor's degree, salaries generally range from about $13,500 to $19,000 per year. Social workers with master's degrees generally earn between $20,000 and $22,000 per year.

Summary

Residential treatment facilities offer many career opportunities for individuals interested in helping people. Numerous and expanding opportunities are available in rehabilitation settings, particularly those that specialize in assisting individuals with multiple problems.

Residential facilities may include group homes or halfway houses that provide specialized programs for persons with mental illness, alcohol and drug abuse problems, criminal records, developmental disabilities, or physical disabilities. These programs serve children, youth, teenagers, and adults who need some supervision or assistance on a day-to-day basis. Some programs of this nature provide a full-time, highly trained staff including house parents, psychologists, medical personnel, rehabilitation counselors, and social workers.

Residential treatment facilities are an alternative to more restrictive environments for individuals who are in the process of recovery or for those who have stabilized but cannot live on their own in the community. Such facilities provide therapy, support, and assistance. Individuals who are interested in careers described in this chapter may wish to visit a residential facility in their community and meet with the various professionals to discuss their respective occupations. Reading materials listed at the end of this chapter provide further information about occupational opportunities in residential treatment facilities.

Further Information

You can obtain additional information from your counselor or career center. You might read the *Occupational Outlook Handbook*, or you could contact the professional associations listed below. Their addresses can be found in the appendix.

Nurse: American Nurses' Association
Occupational Therapist: American Occupational Therapy Association
Physical Therapist: American Physical Therapy Association
Psychologist: American Psychological Association
Rehabilitation Counselor: American Rehabilitation Counseling Association; National Rehabilitation Counseling Association
Recreation Therapist: American Therapeutic Recreation Association; National Council on Therapeutic Recreation; National Parks and Recreation Association
Social Worker: National Association of Social Work
Speech-Language Therapist: American Speech, Language, and Hearing Association

References

Barry, P., & O'Leary, J. (1989). Roles of psychologist on a traumatic injury rehabilitation team. *Rehabilitation Psychology, 34*(2), 83–89.

Golden, C. (1988). Using the Luria-Nebraska Neuropsychological Examination in cognitive rehabilitation. *Cognitive Rehabilitation, 6*(3), 26–30.

Hallauerm, D.S., Prosser, R.A., & Swift, K.F. (1989). Neuropsychological evaluation in the vocational rehabilitation of brain injured clients. *Journal of Applied Rehabilitation Counseling, 20*(2), 3–7.

Leland, M., Lewis, F.D., Hinman, S., & Carrillo, R. (1988). Functional retraining of traumatically brain injured adults in a transdisciplinary environment. *Rehabilitation Counseling Bulletin, 31*(4), 289–297.

McMahon, B.T., Shaw, L.R., & Mahaffey, D.P. (1988). Career opportunities and professional preparation in head injury rehabilitation. *Rehabilitation Counseling Bulletin, 31*(4), 344–354.

Wright, G.N. (1980). *Total rehabilitation*. Boston: Little, Brown.

Chapter 12

CAREERS WORKING WITH SPECIAL POPULATIONS

Barbara Brown Robinson

Many different kinds of groups might be called "special populations." In one sense, each chapter in this book has emphasized a "special population"—school pupils, college students, rehabilitation clients, incarcerated persons, or persons in health care settings. The term *special populations* also refers to people who have a particular need, issue, or concern that would be addressed by counseling or human development professionals. Women, members of ethnic minority groups, persons with handicapping conditions, people who have experienced traumatic events such as sexual assault or childhood abuse, and persons with particular medical conditions are all examples of members of "special populations" who need counseling and human development services.

Services are provided to special populations by professionals who have degrees in counseling, social work, psychology, and related human services fields. Many lay or paraprofessional helpers also may provide assistance; therefore, descriptions of a common professional preparation program is not possible. For the most part, the needs of special populations are the same as those of the general population; however, some aspects of their lives result in unique problems and needs. Frequently, members of special populations prefer assistance from persons who share their life condition; they may feel that a person who has experienced a similar situation is in a better position to understand them and provide the kind of assistance they need.

It is very important to ask yourself how well you believe you would be able to understand and work with persons much different than you are. It is easy to see that if you were to work with a Spanish-speaking student, it would be important to speak Spanish in order to be most helpful; however, what would you need in your own experience or understanding to be of help to persons who were homeless, addicted to drugs or alcohol, culturally different, a different age, or whose values were greatly different than your own? Obviously, the challenge of being an effective professional increases as the group you work with differs more from your own orientation. And the difficulty of the challenge includes two parts: the extra effort you would have to expend to know the group well, and the difficulty you would face in being accepted as a credible helper if you were obviously different than the person you were trying to help.

Many different groups of persons fall into the "special population" category. A few of those groups, and some of the counseling and human development professions to be found working with them, are described below.

Multicultural Populations

The United States has always opened its doors to persons in search of refuge from war, poverty, famine, and political oppression. Indeed, we are a country of immigrants. In recent years there has been an increase in immigration, particularly from Central America, Africa, and Asia. These immigrants' values may differ from those of the community to which they have moved, and their beliefs and practices may not be consistent with those represented by established social and mental health services systems. Public schools and community agencies must decide how best to provide services to new students who may not understand the culture or may speak little or no English.

It is essential to understand the needs and cultural differences of American minorities as well as those of new immigrants. Counselors and helping professionals must be culturally sensitive in order to be professionally skilled. Graduate training programs are requiring counselors, psychologists, social workers, and other mental health professionals to demonstrate competence in multicultural awareness. In some universities, academic majors or degrees can be obtained in multicultural specialties.

There are many opportunities for counseling and human development professionals to work with multicultural populations. Schools, agencies, hospitals, churches, community programs, and special centers all have a demand for professionals who can work effectively with members of different ethnic and racial groups. Professionals might work in colleges or universities as student services personnel who specialize in responding to Black or African-American, Asian, Native American, or Hispanic student needs (see chapter 4). They might be employed in community outreach centers that serve ethnic minority members. These outreach centers might be funded and operated by city or county units (see chapter 8).

Many outreach centers are volunteer organizations that rely on donations or church support for their existence. Other opportunities for counseling and human development professionals who work with multicultural populations can be found in service organizations—scouts, 4-H, or other youth organizations.

New immigrant populations require different kinds of services. Language and cultural differences intensify and complicate delivery of services in most situations. The new immigrant may require more immediate physical assistance with housing, food, clothing, employment, transportation, and compliance with laws and regulations—basic survival needs. Once those needs have been met, issues of emotional well-being can begin to be addressed. It is important for counseling and human development professionals to understand the culture from which the new immigrant comes in order to know what kind of therapeutic assistance is most appropriate. It is also important to understand the cultural norms to foresee what conflicts might arise that would not be difficulties in the professional's culture. Some persons have suggested that the best helper is a person from the same culture; others have pointed out that with special training, professionals can be of help across cultures.

Whether dealing with established American minorities or with new immigrant groups, it may be helpful to have "cultural consultants" who work with counseling and human development professionals to advise them on problems, methods, and delivery systems for special groups. The cultural consultant might be a person from that culture, or a person who has studied the special group extensively and can provide good advice.

Salary

Income for persons working in the variety of multicultural services programs described above could range from nothing (for the many volunteer workers) to high annual incomes associated with positions for psychiatrists or medical directors.

Persons in Crisis

The need to provide immediate services to persons in crisis has led to the development of a number of services including "hot lines" or help lines, outreach care teams (rape or suicide), shelters for the homeless, battered women centers, emergency walk-in services at hospitals and mental health centers, and various support groups. These services are operated by a variety of public and private social service organizations and special interest groups who are concerned with crisis situations including rape, suicide, substance abuse, and family violence.

Hot lines, sometimes called help lines, are telephone numbers that may be called anonymously. You might look in the front of your local telephone book to see if hot-line phone numbers are listed for suicide, runaways, or other crisis situations. The caller speaks to a trained person who can provide crisis counseling and referral. These lines are usually set up to respond to general concerns or to one type of problem such as addiction, child or spouse abuse, suicide, divorce, or rape. The persons who answer the phones are often volunteers with special training. The paid professionals—counselors, psychologists, social workers, psychiatrists, or others—may be the ones responsible for the hot-line operation, for training the volunteers, and for response to the callers whose problems are beyond the ability of the volunteer to assist them.

Shelters for the homeless and for battered and abused spouses provide temporary housing. Other services provided often include referral to appropriate social service agencies, and information regarding housing, day care, food sources, and employment resources.

The professional services mental health teams working in an office or center provide are often supplemented by outreach "care-teams" that will go to the individual who is in crisis. Walk-in or emergency call-in services are often provided on an extended basis, after the normal agency closing hours, in order to provide immediate help for persons in crisis.

Although crisis services are operated by trained professional counselors, social workers, or psychologists, they rely heavily on the assistance of volunteers. Some volunteers are trained to provide direct counseling and referral services. Other volunteers are active as fund-raisers, community advocates, and educators, and can identify resources for client information and referral. Volunteers may be trained in counseling skills, interviewing skills, recognition of immediate need for intervention, and in referral and information sources. They are expected to provide a set number of hours of service per month for a specific period of time.

Salary

Wages for persons who work in crisis centers can also vary from nothing (volunteer service) to substantial (for directors or full-time counselors and therapists) [see chapter 8].

Aging Populations

Currently almost 30 million Americans are 60 years of age or older. Americans are living longer and are more active in their older years.

Because of this, a relatively new field called gerontology has expanded in the last 20 years to meet the special needs of older citizens. The elderly are as diverse as the populations in general and share the concerns and problems common to us all. As we grow older, we have more pronounced needs in certain aspects of our lives. Some of these needs are in the areas of physically accessible housing, retirement and leisure issues, health, employment, nutrition, and protective services.

Services are provided by public, private, and nonprofit agencies through a variety of social service agencies and specialized settings—senior centers, adult care facilities such as day care centers, nursing homes, and nutrition centers.

Counselors, psychologists, and social workers in these settings may also have completed course work or degrees in gerontology. Many gerontological workers may have associate degrees in human services or may have received training through programs developed to educate persons to work with older adults. They have a variety of job titles: senior specialist, caseworker, information and referral specialist, or retirement counselor. These workers help senior citizens by providing assistance in understanding their financial status, benefits for which they may qualify, options for residence, and employment opportunities.

After attention has been given to basic physical needs, professional workers may find that the more personal emotional needs of the gerontological population become a focus for their counseling activities. Issues of aging—diminished physical or mental capacity, changing relationships with family members, loss of marriage partner or close friends, feeling a lack of worth that often comes from a loss of identity following retirement—all become common counseling issues for an aging population.

Gerontological specialists may provide assistance in counseling and support groups. They also may provide aid through information and referral services that help to identify resources. They may serve as advocates for older workers and widows, assist with family concerns, and help identify protective and other services for adults who are neglected, abused, or incompetent. Particularly in senior centers, they may assist in providing trips, lectures, exercise, social programs, and other leisure activities.

Older citizens often serve as peer counselors, either as paid workers or as volunteers, and facilitate activities such as widow-to-widow programs. These are programs where one person (who has been widowed) might be matched up with one or more other widowed persons to provide companionship and mutual assistance. One goal of such a program would be to enable persons to help each other and not be solely dependent on service agencies.

Salary

Salaries depend on the local situation where employment is found.

Substance Abusers

One of the most difficult problems we currently face in the United States is substance abuse. Almost every one of us knows someone whose life has been affected by the abuse of alcohol or drugs. Programs have been designed for people of all ages to provide education about the dangers of alcohol and drug abuse.

Psychologists, counselors, social workers, and other mental health professionals who work with substance abusers have specialized knowledge about the potential causes, symptoms, and physical and psychological effects of substance abuse. They must also be able to work with the families of substance abusers and with children as well as adults who were raised in families where alcohol or drug abuse was a problem.

Counseling services are often provided by former abusers who have successfully overcome their addictions, and by other paraprofessionals who have received specialized training in providing individual and group counseling.

Treatment is provided on both an inpatient and outpatient basis in a variety of settings, including hospitals, mental health centers, drug and alcohol treatment centers, halfway houses, crisis centers, and schools. Individual and group counseling are often supplemented by involvement in special groups such as Alcoholics or Narcotics Anonymous, Al-Anon, and Al-Ateen. Human development specialists who work with this special population provide individual and group counseling and education programs covering topics such as the physical effects of substance abuse, anger control, stress management, relapse prevention, and interpersonal skills improvement (see chapters 8–11).

Salary

Salaries for substance abuse and addictions counselors range from $14,000 to $23,000 and vary with level of education.

Gender Issues

Since the advent of the Women's Movement in the 1960s, greater attention is being paid to the ways in which gender and sexual orientation affect our lives. Women and men—straight, gay, or lesbian—are all affected by stereotypes, prejudices, and fears that affect how we live our lives.

Psychologists, counselors, and social workers may choose to specialize in women's issues, men's issues, or gay and lesbian issues to provide counseling related to these populations. Concerns may include gender identification, sex roles in the family, nontraditional family life, parenthood and bonding, and heterosexuality and homosexuality.

These counselors are usually trained in traditional counseling and human development programs and take courses in their particular areas of interest. This is fairly easy in the area of women's issues because many universities have academic majors available in women's studies. Academic majors in men's studies, or gay and lesbian studies, are rare—if not nonexistent. Counselors must select from the courses available and supplement their knowledge by individual study and by working in settings that specialize in the counseling of lesbian, gay, or straight men and women.

Counselors who specialize in gender issues may work in special centers, such as women's counseling centers, gay men's health centers, mental health centers, or college and university counseling centers.

Salary

Salaries depend on the work setting (see chapters 4 and 8).

Health and Wellness

Counselors and human development professionals can work with health and wellness issues with two different populations: (a) healthy persons who seek to improve their life situation through diet, stress management, exercise, and personal counseling; and (b) persons who experience a particular illness or disease, such as AIDS, cancer, kidney failure, emphysema, or genetic disorders (e.g., sickle cell anemia, Tay-Sachs disease, Hodgkin's disease, etc). There are opportunities for counselors to work with the healthy just as there are opportunities to work with the ill in order to improve their lives.

Counselors may choose to specialize in an area such as anorexia and bulimia or may provide individual or group counseling and education on life-style issues such as stress, poor eating practices, and substance abuse. Health counselors may also choose to work with a population with specific medical concerns. Counseling positions exist in reproductive health centers, community health agencies, or neighborhood medical centers.

Health and wellness counselors must be knowledgeable about health issues and frequently combine studies in nursing and public health with courses in counseling. They provide accurate information on health concerns, identify resources and sources of information, and provide individual and group counseling. Peer counselors and self-help groups are common in this area.

Paraprofessionals and volunteers should be carefully screened and trained in counseling skills. Volunteers may also provide assistance in program development, planning and conducting educational workshops, and making public presentations.

Salary

Salaries depend on the work setting (see chapter 10).

Special Need Agencies

There are a number of special agencies where counseling and human development professions are in demand. Both public and private agencies respond to special needs. The counseling positions in special need agencies may be available to volunteers, to part-time employees, or to full-time trained and licensed professionals. In part, the availability of jobs would depend on the size of the community, the mission of the agency, and the level of funding available.

An example of an agency with a special focus would be Planned Parenthood. Often agencies of this kind, which deal with special concerns, may have a strong position on what are acceptable and unacceptable outcomes for clients. It is important for the client who goes to such an agency to know the agency's philosophy on issues of concern to them. It is also important for individuals who want a career in counseling with an agency to understand both the agency's and their own personal philosophy in order to have compatibility of personal philosophy and agency mission. Counselors who work at one agency where unwanted pregnancy is a common issue may find that they are urged to persuade clients to take a particular course of action—perhaps delivery and adoption without mention of abortion alternatives. At a different agency, counselors may be encouraged to present a full range of options to clients and take no stand on the decision to be made.

It is important that you understand your own values before becoming a counseling professional—especially when the work setting you would be in would be a value-oriented agency. It is equally important that you understand the value orientation of the agency you would work for.

Summary

It is truly challenging and rewarding to be a helper with special populations. The many persons who can be described as members of a "special population" have specific needs that must be addressed. The helping professionals who can develop the levels of awareness, sensitivity, and skill necessary to work effectively with persons in these groups—especially when the group's orientation differs from their own—demonstrate some of the highest levels of professional performance in counseling and human development careers. This could be an exciting career area to explore.

Further Information

Your counselor or career center can provide you with information about opportunities in working with special populations. Some of the associations that center on the needs of a few of the groups mentioned in this chapter are listed below. The addresses can be found in the appendix if you choose to write them.

> *Aging*: Association for Adult Development and Aging; American Association of Retired Persons
> *Gender Issues*: American Association for Counseling and Development (Committee on Gay, Lesbian, and Bisexual Issues in Counseling); American Psychological Association (Committee on Women)
> *Multicultural Populations*: Association for Multicultural Counseling and Development
> *Persons in Crisis*: American Association for Counseling and Development; American Psychological Association; National Association of Social Work

Part III

Moving Ahead

The last section of this book provides suggestions about what to do next if you are interested in pursuing one or more of the career options described in the work-setting chapters. Chapter 13, "Credentialing, Certification, and Licensure," is important for you to understand as you make decisions about careers in counseling and human development. Some of the information in chapter 13 is the kind that you would want to have before making a decision about an educational program you would enter; some is the kind that would be relevant only if you were in a state that licenses professionals in a field that you plan to enter. You will have to do more work after reading this chapter in order to apply the information to your own situation.

Chapter 14, "What Next," gives you some hints about the next steps you could take in your own career decision process. It makes the assumption that you have read the opening chapters in part 1 and one or more of the chapters in part 2.

Following chapter 14 are supplementary materials that can help you in your "next steps." You will find a list of associations and organizations mentioned in one or more places in the book. These associations can be contacted for additional information on occupations you wish to pursue in depth. You will also find an alphabetical list of all the occupations mentioned in the book and a page reference where each mention occurs. For example, if you have found that you are interested in the occupational title *consultant*, which you read about in one chapter, you might look at the other places in the book where that same title was used.

A third resource for you is the "Matrix of Occupational Titles and Work Settings." Like the index, this will show you which work settings included specific occupational titles; however, many occupational titles not described in the work-setting chapters may be found in the various work settings. The matrix will give you both kinds of information. As an example, the occupation *Rehabilitation Counselor* is described in chapters 7, 9, 10, and 11. Rehabilitation counselors also work in public and private agencies (chapter 8). The matrix will show that kind of information.

How do you move ahead? You do it one step at a time. Reading this book is a big step. We hope that your next steps are made easier by the information you have here. Good wishes.

Chapter 13

CREDENTIALING, CERTIFICATION, AND LICENSURE

Judy Rosenbaum and Sharon J. Alexander

Before you consult any professionals—medical, legal, financial, or mental health—how do you assess their competence? One way to start is to ask for information about their training and the standards they have met. The questions that informed consumers are likely to ask include the following: Did they attend an accredited institution? Are they licensed? Are they certified? Positive responses to these questions indicate that they have met minimum standards established for their profession. You should know about each of these standards, not only to be better informed consumers, but also to guide you as you examine the standards for mental health professionals. You should use the same important information in making your own decision about a professional career.

We will talk about three types of credentialing: (a) accreditation, (b) licensure, and (c) certification. To best introduce you to the various aspects of credentialling, Table 1 identifies the process, whom it affects, whether it is mandatory or voluntary, and who is the regulator.

Accreditation

All educational institutions, from elementary schools to universities, are encouraged to obtain accreditation. To become accredited, an institution must meet established standards set by a regional accrediting agency. The primary purpose of accreditation is to promote and ensure the quality of training programs. A commonly accepted standard for later employment, further graduate work, or the ability to become licensed or certified

TABLE 1

Key Factors in Credentialing

Process	Impacts	Participation	Regulator
Accreditation	Higher ed institutions & specialty departments	Voluntary	Regional accreditation agencies & national accreditation bodies
Licensure	Individuals	Mandatory	State legislature
National certification	Individuals	Voluntary	National certification agencies
State certification	Individuals	Mandatory	State department of education; state certifying board

is that your degree be granted by an institution that is regionally accredited. Your eligibility for federal loan assistance or transferring academic credits often depends upon this recognition. Most higher education institutions have some kind of accreditation.

The academic accreditation process begins with an intensive self-evaluation to assess an institution, its stated objectives, and standards. Information about students, faculty qualifications, courses offered, student-teacher ratio, number of counselors and other staff, and many other items of information are gathered and sent to a review committee. A site visit is then made by a team of professional peers representing the accrediting body to obtain additional information and to see the educational institution in operation.

In addition to obtaining accreditation for an entire institution, some individual university departments may apply for and obtain accreditation for their particular specialty. For example, the fields of counseling, psychology, and social work all have accrediting organizations that set minimum standards for these programs. Accrediting organizations are listed in one section of the Appendix. If you select a program that has been accredited by one of these credentialing bodies, your degree will be valued more and you will be more likely to be considered for licensure or certification. Most counseling, psychology, and social work programs are located at regionally accredited colleges and universities, although some programs are offered in special institutes or centers.

Although most institutions that are eligible to seek regional, system-wide accreditation do so, specific departments do not always make this choice. Some professionals believe that this process places restrictions or requirements on their departments that are not necessary. Some departments cannot meet the requirements. Standards for training mental health professionals are influenced by professional organizations that represent the various specialties. These include the American Association for Counseling and Development (AACD), the American Association for Marriage and Family Therapy (AAMFT), the American Association for Pastoral Counselors (AAPC), the American Psychological Association (APA), and the National Association of Social Workers (NASW). Each of these organizations is affiliated with specialized accrediting agencies that provide the opportunity for programs to be reviewed and recognized by professional peers.

As a student choosing a graduate program of study, you will find it important to know what credentialing standards your institution and program have or have not met. Although accreditation is a voluntary process, programs that are not accredited often have difficulty attracting students.

Licensure

In contrast to accreditation, which is granted to educational institutions, licensure is a legal status granted to individuals. Physicians and lawyers must be licensed to practice in their state. The requirements for licensure for the different mental health specialties vary by specialty and by state. In most states, in order to represent yourself as a professional counselor, psychologist, or social worker, you must be licensed. Other states have this requirement for some or none of these mental health professionals. Some states require licensure only for those who are in private practice. Mental health professionals who work in institutional settings (such as schools, mental health centers, hospitals, etc.) may need to meet agency requirements rather than state licensure standards. No simple answer applies to licensure of mental health professionals in all states. Because the recent trend is for states to pass licensure laws, you should seriously consider requirements for this credential when choosing a graduate preparation program. It is important to keep your employment options as broad as possible.

The minimum requirement for licensure as a counselor or social worker is a master's degree from a regionally accredited university. Licensure as a psychologist requires a doctorate in most states. Specific coursework, supervised experience, and passing an examination are additional requirements. As of September 1989, 32 states had passed licensure laws for counselors, and 34 states license social workers. All states have passed licensure laws regulating psychologists. Listed in the Appendix are organizations that can help you get information about current regulations.

National Certification

National certification is also a credential for individuals. Because it is national in scope, it will be recognized in any part of the country. Like licensure, it requires the individual to have an advanced degree from an accredited institution, pass an examination, and have worked as a mental health professional for a certain period of time (usually 2 years). Certification does not give you the authority to practice. If there is a licensure regulation in the state, you must meet that requirement. Although national certification is not a mandatory credential, it does indicate to employers and clients that you have met minimum standards established by your profession.

Professional Associations

The appendix lists many different professional associations. Each association has members who are helpers in the counseling and human development field. A professional association is an organization of persons who have something in common—either their occupation, their training, their work setting, or the way they practice their profession. The association is a place where members share ideas about what they do through print- and nonprint media as well as through meetings, conferences, and conventions of various kinds. The occupation or career area that might interest you in counseling and human development is probably represented among the associations listed in the appendix. You could write that association for additional information.

Accreditation and Certifying Bodies

You will also find several accrediting and certifying bodies listed in the appendix. Those groups have specific information about how you can become a certified professional or how an educational program becomes accredited. If you have questions about either of these topics, the organizations listed could provide specific information for you.

Some Final Thoughts

Becoming and being part of any profession is a lifelong endeavor. Your degree provides a foundation for continued growth through reading, workshops, conferences, and special courses. Although some problems helping professionals face remain constant, other aspects are constantly changing. New problems and treatment approaches mean that the mental health field is always changing; being engaged in it can be challenging, interesting, and personally rewarding.

Professional associations play an important role in helping mental health professionals stay current in their field. They produce newsletters, journals, and other publications to help members learn about new developments. They also provide training, influence legislation and public policy, and develop codes of ethics to guide professional behavior.

Whatever field you select, the credentials of the training program you attend will be important in the quality of training you receive. Licensure or certification will be important to your development and recognition as a professional. Be sure to investigate the accreditation of any program you consider. Then, as you develop as a professional, seek certification or licensure. Finally, inform your employers and potential clients about your training and professional credentials.

Further Information

The two following books provide good information on many topics discussed in this chapter:

Hollis, J.W., & Wantz, R.A. (1986). *Counselor preparation 1986–1989: Programs, personnel, and trends* (6th ed.). Muncie, IN: Accelerated Development.

Vacc, N.A., & Loesch, L.C. (1987). *Counseling as a profession*. Muncie, IN: Accelerated Development.

Chapter 14

WHAT NEXT?

Nancy J. Garfield and Brooke B. Collison

As you have read through this book you have learned much about counseling and human development careers and the career search process. You began by learning about the general characteristics or qualities of people who work in the helping professions and what types of educational progams and requirements there are for the counseling and human development fields. You then had the opportunity to explore 10 different work settings where counselors and human development specialists work. You learned of professional opportunities that exist for individuals who wish to work with and help people. You also learned about credentialing and accreditation, the importance of accreditation of academic departments and training programs, and about the value of being a credentialed provider in those fields that encourage or require credentialing.

After all that reading, you may still be unsure about a specific occupational choice. This is a good time to review the checklist you completed in chapter 2. You may wish to use this information in talking with a counselor about occupations you are considering.

Talking with a counselor can provide you with an opportunity to learn more about yourself and your interests. You and your counselor may want to consider whether you could learn more about yourself by taking an interest inventory. Interest inventories are multiple-choice assessment instruments that compare your likes and dislikes to those of people in a variety of different occupations. People with similar interests usually enjoy and succeed at the same types of occupations. Although interest inventories do not include all the occupations that have been discussed in this book, a number of them are included. Talk with a counselor about your likes and dislikes and what you are good at doing. Do you like to talk with people, listen to people, solve problems, or work with your hands to make or fix things? How much school are you willing to attend? You also need to consider what subjects you do best in academically.

Making an occupational choice also involves learning about what is important to you. Discuss what type of work you like. Would you enjoy working regular hours, days, or nights? Do you like a job where you can wear casual clothes such as blue jeans, or would you prefer a job where you had to wear dressy clothes like a suit or dress most of the time? How much money do you think you will need to live in the style you would like?

If you think that one or more of the areas or occupations described in this book would interest you, you could do several things: You could read the materials referenced in the chapter or chapters about your career choice; you could write to the professional associations listed in the appendix; you could also talk with people who are working in those occupations. Find out what they do during their work week and how much time they spend working with clients, doing paperwork or report writing, consulting with others about their clients, or doing other tasks. Ask them what they like best and least about their jobs. Find out what they think is the future of their profession, what they think people in their field will be doing in 10 or 20 years. Ask to spend some time with them acting as a shadow to see what they do (this may not be possible in the confidential or private nature of many counseling and human development jobs). Many tasks and experiences could provide you with a better sense of the field, and would help you determine if you want to join the profession.

Another way you can learn more about the helping professions is to find summer or part-time work in a field related to your interests. This experience will help you decide if your expressed occupational choice will be a good one for you, one that you will enjoy and find satisfying, and one that will provide you with the personal and financial rewards important to you. Within most schools you can find opportunities to work as an aide in a guidance office or a career center, as a tutor, or as a peer helper.

So what do you do now that you have all this information? Part of that decision depends on where you are in your academic program or career. If you are a high school student or just beginning your college program, select a field or major that will afford you the opportunity to get a good liberal arts education. It should include English composition to enable you to write clearly and well for the reports you will need to complete; a solid grounding in mathematics; and courses in psychology and sociology to help you begin to understand people. For the most part you will need training beyond a bachelor's degree to work in the fields discussed in this book.

Some careers require special undergraduate majors. School counseling (see chapter 3) is an example. Most states require school counselors to have been certified and experienced as teachers before they can be school counselors. If you are thinking about a professional career that has specific educational major requirements at the undergraduate level, check those out before you move too far in a different academic major.

If you have completed your undergraduate degree, you will need to choose a graduate degree program that will enable you to do the type of work you have identified as your career choice. When you decide which work setting and which occupation you wish to pursue, then you will need to select a graduate school and course of study that will enable you to enter that profession. As you have read, many occupations require a master's degree and others require a doctorate (PhD, PsyD, or EdD). You will need to ascertain what type of degree will be required for your occupational choice. Talk to people already in that profession, faculty at schools you are considering, and the state agencies that license or certify the profession you have chosen. Get information from the professional organizations of your career choice about what the minimum educational and credentialing requirements are for that occupation.

Applying to Graduate Programs

Students generally need a 2.7 to a 3.0 minimum undergraduate grade point average, and at least the 50th percentile on a standardized test such as the Graduate Record Exam (GRE) or Miller's Analogies Test (MAT) for graduate school admission. Provisional admission may be possible if a student does not meet these standard requirements but can demonstrate other talents and strengths. Requirements vary in different graduate programs. Graduate applications need to be made by February or March for fall enrollment and to seek graduate assistantships to work on campus. Many programs require a personal interview. Interested students should write both the graduate school to obtain an application and catalog and the program of interest to obtain curriculum guides, brochures, or assistantship information. Each program usually has a faculty admission committee, and you may want to call or visit to learn more about the program. Sometimes more information on specific areas of graduate study can be obtained from professional associations. For example, the American College Personnel Association publishes a directory of many graduate preparation programs that includes entrance requirements and sample courses (see Kiem & Graham, 1987, in "Recommended Readings" at the end of chapter 4).

Graduate assistantships are often available for students enrolled in professional study. They are usually 20-hour-per-week work obligations that provide modest income and usually include a tuition waiver for graduate credits. On most campuses prospective students apply for graduate assistantships like they would for any job. Assistantships are meaningful work experiences in such areas as residence life or academic advising.

These are all topics to discuss with a counselor. Making a career choice is a process that involves learning about yourself and about the work world. Making a choice is a process that takes time. You must learn about what is important to you: what your values, your personal priorities, and your abilities are, and what personality characteristics you have that would or would not fit the occupations you are considering.

The next step is yours—It could be a big one. Good wishes.

PROFESSIONAL ASSOCIATIONS, CERTIFYING GROUPS, AND ACCREDITING AGENCIES

Professional Associations

American Art Therapy Association, Inc.
505 East Hawley St.
Mundelein, IL 66660

American Association for Adult and Continuing Education
1112 16th St., N.W.
Suite 420
Washington, DC 20036

American Association for Counseling and Development
5999 Stevenson Avenue
Alexandria, VA 22304

American Association for Marriage and Family Therapy
1717 K Street, N.W.
Washington, DC 20006

American Association for Music Therapy
66 Morris Ave.
Springfield, NJ 07081

American Association of Pastoral Counselors
9508A Lee Highway
Fairfax, VA 22301

American College Personnel Association
5999 Stevenson Avenue
Alexandria, VA 22304

American Correctional Association
4321 Hartwick Rd., Suite L208
College Park, MD 20740

American Dance Therapy Association
2000 Century Plaza, Suite 108
Columbia, MD 21044

American Mental Health Counselors Association
5999 Stevenson Avenue
Alexandria, VA 22304

American Nurses' Association
2420 Pershing Road
Kansas City, MO 64108

American Psychological Association
1200 17th St., N.W.
Washington, DC 20036

American Rehabilitation Counseling Association
5999 Stevenson Avenue
Alexandria, VA 22304

American School Counseling Association
5999 Stevenson Avenue
Alexandria, VA 22304

American Society for Group Psychotherapy and Psychodrama
6728 Old McLean Village Dr.
McLean, VA 22101

American Speech, Language, and Hearing Association
10801 Rockville Pike
Rockville, MD 20852

American Therapeutic Recreation Association
2021 L. Street, N.W.
Washington, DC 20036

Association for Adult Development and Aging
5999 Stevenson Avenue
Alexandria, VA 22304

Association for Counselor Education and Supervision
5999 Stevenson Avenue
Alexandria, VA 22304

Association for Multicultural Counseling and Development
5999 Stevenson Avenue
Alexandria, VA 22304

Association of College and University Housing Officers International
101 Curl Drive, Suite 140
Columbus, OH 43210

Association of State Boards of Psychology
55 So. Prairie Street
Montgomery, AL 36103

Federal Probation Officers Association
U.S. Probation Office
Box 432
Burlington, VT 05402

International Association of Counseling Services
5999 Stevenson Avenue
Alexandria, VA 22304

International Association of Marriage and Family Counseling
5999 Stevenson Avenue
Alexandria, VA 22304

Military Educators and Counselors Association
5999 Stevenson Avenue
Alexandria, VA 22304

National Association for Campus Activities
P.O. Box 6828
Columbia, SC 29260

National Association for Dance Therapy
19 Edwards St.
New Haven, CT 06511

National Association for Music Therapy
505 11th St., S.E.
Washington, DC 20003

National Association for Poetry Therapy
225 Williams St.
Huron, OH 44839

National Association for Women Deans, Administrators, & Counselors
1325 18th St., N.W., #210
Washington, DC 20036

National Association of Social Workers
7981 Eastern Avenue
Silver Spring, MD 20910

National Association of Student Personnel Administrators
Elizabeth Nuss, Executive Director
1700 18th St., N.W., Suite 301
Washington, DC 20009-2508

National Career Development Association
5999 Stevenson Avenue
Alexandria, VA 22304

National Council on Therapeutic Recreation
49 Main St.
Suite 005
Spring Valley, NY 10977

National Employment Counselors Association
5999 Stevenson Avenue
Alexandria, VA 22304

National Parks and Recreation Association
Division of Professional Services
3101 Park Center Drive
Alexandria, VA 22302

National Rehabilitation Counseling Association
633 S. Washington St.
Alexandria, VA 22314

National Therapeutic Recreation Society
3101 Park Center Drive
Alexandria, VA 22302

National Orientation Directors Association
Ray Passkiewicz, Associate Dean
Davenport College
4123 W. Main St.
Kalamazoo, MI 49007-2791

National Therapeutic Recreation Society
3101 Park Center Drive
Alexandria, VA 22302

Public Offender Counselor Association
5999 Stevenson Avenue
Alexandria, VA 22304

Certifying Groups

Academy of Certified Social Workers
7981 Eastern Ave.
Silver Spring, MD 20910

American Association of State Counseling Boards
c/o Mary Alice Cates, Chair
P.O. Box 3303
Delta State University
Cleveland, MS 38733

American Association of State Psychology Boards
P.O. Box 4389
555 S. Perry St., Suite 112
Montgomery, AL 36103

American Association of State Social Work Boards
718 Arch Street
Philadelphia, PA 19106

American Occupational Therapy Certification Board
1383 Piccard Drive
P.O. Box 1725
Rockville, MD 20850-4375

Certification Board for Music Therapists, Inc.
1133 15th St., N.W.
Suite 1000
Washington, DC 20005

Commission on Rehabilitation Counselor Certification
1156 Shure Dr., Suite 350
Arlington Heights, IL 60004

Council for the National Register of Health Service Providers in
  Psychology
1730 Rhode Island Avenue, N.W.
Suite 1200
Washington, DC 20036

National Academy of Certified Clinical Mental Health Counselors
5999 Stevenson Avenue
Alexandria, VA 22304

National Board for Certified Counselors
5999 Stevenson Avenue
Alexandria, VA 22304

National Council for Therapeutic Recreation Certification
P.O. Box 16126
Alexandria, VA 22302

NASW Register of Clinical Social Workers
7981 Estern Avenue
Silver Spring, MD 20910

National League for Nursing
10 Columbus Circle
New York, NY 10019

Accrediting Agencies

American Psychological Association
1200 17th St., N.W.
Washington, DC 20036

Council for Accreditation of Counseling and Related Educational
    Programs
5999 Stevenson Avenue
Alexandria, VA 22304

Council on Rehabilition Education
185 N. Wabash
Room 1617
Chicago, IL 60601

Council on Social Work Education
1744 R. St, N.W.
Washington, DC 20009

Appendix B

MATRIX OF OCCUPATIONAL
TITLES AND WORK SETTINGS

JOB TITLE/ OCCUPATION	License (L) Certification (C) MAY BE Required	WORK SETTING									
		School Counseling	Post-Secondary Institutions	Higher Ed Consulting	Business & Industry	Private Practice	Public & Private Agencies	Federal & State Agencies	Health Care Facilities	Residential Treatment Centers	Special Populations
Academic Advisor			●								
Administrator		●	○		●	○	●	○	●	○	○
Admissions Counselor			●								
Black Student Advisor		○	●								○
Business Manager			●		○	○	○	○	○	○	
Career Consultant			●	○	○	○					
Career Counselor			●	●	○	●	○	○	○	○	○
Case Manager						●	○	●	○	●	○
Case Worker			●				○	○	○	○	●
Chancellor			●								
Clinical Mental Health Counselor	C		○		○	●	●	○	○	○	○
Coach			●								

Continued

WORK SETTING

JOB TITLE/ OCCUPATION	License (L) Certification (C) MAY BE Required	School Counseling	Post-Secondary Institutions	Higher Ed Consulting	Business & Industry	Private Practice	Public & Private Agencies	Federal & State Agencies	Health Care Facilities	Residential Treatment Centers	Special Populations
Consultant			●	●	○	●	○	○	●	○	●
Consulting Psychologist	L		○	●	○	○	○	○	○	○	
Coordinator of Freshman Experience			●								
Coordinator of Special Services	L/C		●								
Correction Counselor/Psychologist	L/C							●			
Counselor	C	●	●	●	●	●	●	●	●	●	●
Cultural Consultant			○	○							●
Dance Therapist	C								●	○	
Dean of Admissions			●								
Dean of Freshmen			●								
Dean of Student Affairs			●								
Director of Academic Advising			●								
Director of Athletics			●								
Director of Campus Activities			●								
Director of Career Planning			●								
Director of Commuter Programs			●								
Director of Counseling	L/C	●	●				○	○	○	○	
Director of Greek Life			●								
Director of Housing			●								
Director of Judicial Programs			●								

Role	Code
Director of Learning Skills Center	
Director of Minority Programs	
Director of Orientation	
Director of Residence Life	
Director of Student Union	
EAP Professional	
Employment Counselor	
Employment Interviewer	
Employment Recruiter	
Family Counselor	
Gerontological Counselor	
Head Resident/Hall Director	L
Health Psychologist	
Human Resources Manager	
Hypnotherapist	
International Student Advisor	
Learning Skills Specialist	
Licensed Professional Counselor	L
Mediation Counselor	L/C
Mental Health Counselor	
Military Counselor	C
Music Therapist	L
Neuropsychologist	L
Nurse	L

Continued

WORK SETTING

JOB TITLE/OCCUPATION	License (L) Certification (C) MAY BE Required	School Counseling	Post-Secondary Institutions	Higher Ed Consulting	Business & Industry	Private Practice	Public & Private Agencies	Federal & State Agencies	Health Care Facilities	Residential Treatment Centers	Special Populations
Occupational Therapist	L						○	○	●	●	
Parole Officer								●			
Personnel Manager	L	○	○		●		○	○	○	○	
Physical Therapist	L								○	●	
Physician	L	○	○		○	○	○	○	●	●	○
President			●		○						
Probation Officer								●			
Professional Counselor	L/C	●	○	○	○	●	●	○	○	○	●
Psychiatric Aide	C					●	●	○	●	○	
Psychiatrist	L	●	○		○	○	●	○	●	○	○
Psychologist (Clinical, Counseling)	L	●	●	●	○	●	●	●	●	●	●
Psychology Technician						○	○	○	●	○	
Psychometrist			●			○	○	○	○	○	
Psychotherapist			●			●		○	●	○	○
Recreation Therapist/Aide	L/C		●							●	
Registrar	C										
Rehabilitation Counselor	C					●	○	●	●	●	○
Retirement Counselor					○	○	○	○	○		○
School Counselor	C	●									●
School Psychologist	L/C	●									

160

Senior Specialist

Social Worker (Clinical, School)   L

Student Employment Coordinator   C

Substance Abuse Counselor

Teacher

Therapist

Training Director

Training Specialist

Vice President

Vocational Rehabilitation Counselor   C

Wellness Counselor

Youth Services Worker

● indicates occupations that are discussed in that chapter

○ indicates occupations that exist in that work setting but are not discussed in that chapter

CONTRIBUTORS

SHARON J. ALEXANDER is Associate Director for Mental Health Education for the Charlotte Area Health Education Center in Charlotte, NC. She plans continuing education programs and provides consultation services and technical assistance. Dr. Alexander was previously Director of Professional Development and Research at the American Association for Counseling and Development. She has also worked as a school counselor and a high school English teacher. Sharon Alexander received a PhD in family relations from Florida State University in Tallahassee.

BURT BERTRAM is a Florida-Licensed Mental Health Counselor and Marriage and Family Therapist. He has been in private practice in the Orlando, Florida area since 1976. He is also a part-time faculty member in the Counselor Education Program at the University of Central Florida. In addition to counseling, Dr. Bertram consults and provides training to organizations and businesses regarding human relations concerns. Burt Bertram has a doctorate in counseling from the University of Florida.

CLAIRE G. COLE is a former teacher of English and high school and middle school counselor. Currently the editor of *The School Counselor*, she is active in the American School Counselor Association, the National Middle School Association, and the National Association of Secondary School Principals. She is Director, Southwest Virginia Regional Principals Assessment Center. Claire Cole has a doctorate from Virginia Tech.

BROOKE B. COLLISON is associate professor of counseling and guidance at the Oregon State University. He was formerly a counselor educator at The Wichita State University and has experience as a school counselor at both the junior high and senior high school levels. He is a member of the American Association for Counseling and Development and served as president in 1987–1988. Brooke Collison received a PhD in counseling psychology from the University of Missouri-Columbia.

CLYDE A. CREGO is licensed as a psychologist in several states. He is Director of the Counseling Center at California State University, Long Beach, and graduate faculty member in counseling at USC. He maintains an extensive consulting practice to numerous organizations, especially universities and colleges. A Fellow of the American Psychological Association, he is past-president of the Division of Consulting Psychology, and a long-time member of AACD and APA. Clyde Crego received a PhD in clinical psychology from Michigan State University.

NANCY J. GARFIELD is Director of Training and a staff psychologist at the Colmery-O'Neil Veterans Administration Medical Center in Topeka, Kansas. Previous positions include Associate Dean of Student Life and Service at The Wichita State University and counselor/career specialist at Oklahoma State University. Dr. Garfield is a member of the American Association for Counseling and Development and is a representative to AACD Governing Council from the American College Personnel Association. Nancy Garfield received her PhD in counseling psychology from the University of Missouri-Columbia.

BREE HAYES is a counseling psychologist and organizational consultant working in the areas of consultation, education, health promotion, and employee assistance. She is a member of the American Association for Counseling and Development, American Psychological Association, and American Society for Training and Development. Formerly the president of a consulting firm, she is now an assistant professor at the University of Georgia. Bree Hayes received a doctorate in counseling psychology from Boston University.

ANDREW A. HELWIG is an associate professor in counseling and personnel services in the School of Education at the University of Colorado at Denver. Prior to his academic career, he worked as an employment counselor and state counseling supervisor with the Job Service in Wisconsin. He is a National Certified Counselor and a National Certified Career Counselor. Dr. Helwig is an AACD Governing Council member and past president of the National Employment Counselors Association. Andrew Helwig received his PhD in counselor education from the University of Wisconsin-Madison.

SUSAN R. KOMIVES is an assistant professor in counseling and personnel services and faculty associate in the Division of Student Affairs at the University of Maryland-College Park. Previously she has been Vice President for Student Development at the University of Tampa and Stephens College, and has held other student affairs positions at Denison University and the University of Tennessee. She is past president of the American College Personnel Association. Susan Komives received a doctorate in educational administration and supervision from the University of Tennessee-Knoxville.

ROSS K. LYNCH is a rehabilitation psychologist and president of Professional Rehabilitation Services, Ltd., a multidisciplinary rehabilitation clinic located in Madison, Wisconsin. Dr. Lynch is the current president of the American Rehabilitation Counseling Association. Ross Lynch received a PhD in rehabilitation counseling psychology from the University of Wisconsin-Madison.

ROBERT A. MALE has worked as a teacher and school counselor and as a counselor educator. He maintains a private counseling practice, works as a counselor/consultant in vocational rehabilitation, and consults on counseling and vocational matters. Dr. Male is president-elect of the Oregon Counseling Association, and a member of the American Association for Counseling and Development. He received his PhD in counseling and guidance from the University of Wisconsin-Madison.

JOSEPH McCORMACK is a staff psychologist at Colmery-O'Neil Veterans Administration Medical Center in Topeka, Kansas. He is adjunct assistant professor at Washburn University and also has a limited private practice. In the past he has worked for the State of Kansas Reception and Diagnostic Center. He is licensed as a psychologist in Kansas and Missouri and is a member of the American Psychological Association and the Society for Personality Assessment. Joseph McCormack received his PhD in counseling psychology from the University of Missouri-Columbia.

BARBARA BROWN ROBINSON is a visiting scholar with the Washington, DC, branch of the NAACP. She recently served as the Director of Association Relations for the American Association for Counseling and Development. She was formerly the director of preservice and graduate teacher education at the Chicago campus of the National College of Education, a project director for CEMREL, Inc. in St. Louis, and has 20 years of experience in education, counseling, training, and curriculum development—particularly in multicultural issues and counseling of special populations. Barbara Brown Robinson received a PhD in educational psychology-counseling from the University of Illinois at Urbana-Champaign.

JUDY ROSENBAUM is a senior management analyst and executive assistant to the district administrator for the State of Florida Department of Health and Rehabilitative Services. Prior to moving to Florida, Dr. Rosenbaum served as Executive Director of the National Board for Certified Counselors and was also on the executive staff of the American Association for Counseling and Development. She has been a dean of women, an assistant director of housing, a field executive for the Girl Scouts, and a school counselor at both the elementary and secondary levels. Judy Rosenbaum received her doctorate in counselor education from Virginia Tech.

SUSAN M. WIEGMANN is a vocational evaluator at Goodwill Industries in Madison, Wisconsin, and is a doctoral student in rehabilitation counseling psychology. She has worked as a vocational rehabilitation counselor in a return-to-work program and as a job coach in a supported employment program. She is a member of the American Association for Counseling and Development and the National Rehabilitation Association. Susan Wiegmann received her MS in rehabilitation psychology from the University of Wisconsin-Madison and is a certified rehabilitation counselor.

INDEX OF OCCUPATIONAL TITLES
USED IN THIS BOOK

Academic advisor, 37, 40, 50
Administrator, 4, 23, 27, 31, 38, 47, 52–54, 62–64, 85, 94, 97, 111
Admissions counselor, 39
Athletic advisor, 40
Behavioral specialist, 96, 125
Black student advisor, 44
Business manager, 45
Career consultant, 40
Career counselor, 40, 64–66, 73, 92
Case manager, 5, 93, 95, 97, 101, 125–126
Case worker, 133
Chancellor, 38
Clinical behavioral specialist, 96
Clinical director, 84–87
Clinical mental health counselor, 76, 84
Clinical psychologist, 42, 55, 84, 91, 107
Clinical social worker, 84, 87
Clinical supervisor, 88
Coach, 39–40
Consultant, 13, 16–17, 40–41, 49–52, 54–57, 64–65, 68–69, 72–74, 108, 131
Consulting psychologist, 54
Coordinator of freshman experience, 45
Coordinator of special services, 37
Correction counselor, 91, 94–96
Correction psychologist, 5, 91, 94–96
Counseling psychologist, 42, 51, 82, 96, 107

Counselor, 4–8, 10, 12, 14, 16–17, 19, 22–30, 34, 37, 39–43, 46–
    47, 49–51, 53–54, 58–59, 61–66, 70, 72–78, 80–82, 84–98,
    100–104, 106–107, 109, 112, 119–120, 122, 125–128, 130–137,
    140, 142–143, 145, 147–148, 150
Counselor educator, 34, 75, 107
Crisis specialist, 88
Cultural consultant, 131
Dance therapist, 109–110, 119
Dean of admissions, 39, 43
Dean of freshmen, 45
Dean of student affairs, 38
Dean of students, 42–43
Director of academic advising, 37
Director of athletics, 40
Director of campus activities, 46
Director of career planning, 40
Director of commuter programs, 41
Director of counseling, 27, 42
Director of Greek life, 46
Director of housing, 45
Director of judicial programs, 43
Director of learning skills center, 37
Director of minority programs, 44
Director of orientation, 45
Director of residence life, 42
Director of student union, 46
EAP administrator, 62–64
EAP counselor, 62–64
Educational services officer, 102
Educational services specialist, 102
EEO manager, 67–68
Elementary school counselor, 23
Employee services manager, 67
Employment counselor, 92–94
Employment interviewer, 66–67
Employment recruiter, 66
Executive director, 87
Family counselor, 73
Family therapist, 72
Gerontological counselor, 73, 133
Gerontological specialist, 133
Guidance counselor, 2, 102
Hall director, 45

Head resident, 45
Health psychologist, 107–109
Helping professional, 5, 10–11, 33, 61, 70, 83, 130, 136, 145
Human resources manager, 68
Human services worker, 55, 57, 91
Hypnotherapist, 73
International student advisor, 44
Job service representative, 92
Job service specialist, 92
Learning skills specialist, 37
Licensed practical nurse (LPN), 114–115
Licensed professional counselor, 24, 73, 84
Management consultant, 74
Mediation counselor, 73
Mental health counselor, 73, 76, 80, 84
Mental health specialist, 82, 84, 106, 119
Middle school counselor, 23, 25
Military counselor, 91, 102–104
Music therapist, 109–111, 120
Neuropsychologist, 124
Nurse, 5, 24, 32, 34, 82, 84, 106, 108, 112–115, 120, 126, 128
Occupational therapist, 117–118, 122–123, 128
Organizational consultant, 69
Outplacement counselor, 65–66
Parole officer, 91, 94, 98–100, 104
Pastoral counselor, 143
Peer counselor, 88, 133, 136
Personal adjustment counselor, 126
Personnel manager, 68
Physical therapist, 5, 122–123, 128
Physician, 34, 71, 100, 108, 113–115, 119, 122, 143
President, 38–39, 43, 47
Private practitioner, 5, 62, 71–80
Probation officer, 98, 104
Professional counselor, 24, 73, 84, 143
Program coordinator, 85, 88
Program director, 85
Psychiatric aide, 82, 84, 106, 115–116
Psychiatrist, 24, 41, 72, 82–84, 94, 106, 112, 132
Psychological services associate, 91, 96
Psychologist, 23–24, 30, 41–42, 49–52, 54–55, 59, 62, 70, 72–73,
    76, 80, 82–84, 91, 94–97, 100, 106–109, 111–112, 120, 122–124,
    127–128, 130, 132–135, 143

Psychology technician, 111
Psychometrist, 42
Psychotherapist, 73
Recreation aide, 40
Recreation therapist, 94, 118–120, 124, 128
Registered nurse (RN), 114–115, 126
Registrar, 39
Rehabilitation counselor, 73, 76, 89, 91, 100–102, 104–106, 116–117, 120, 122, 125–128, 140
Retirement counselor, 133
School counselor, 22–30, 120
School guidance counselor, 3
School psychologist, 30
School social worker, 30
Senior specialist, 133
Social worker, 8, 24, 30, 70, 72–73, 76, 84, 87, 100, 106, 108, 112–113, 120, 127–128, 130, 132, 143
Student affairs professional, 47
Student employment coordinator, 44
Substance abuse counselor, 5, 24
Teacher, 16, 21, 24–27, 30, 72, 94, 97–98
Therapist, 8, 72–73, 94, 98, 106, 109–111, 117–120, 122–124, 128, 132, 142, 148
Training director, 42, 45
Training specialist, 68
Vice president, 38, 43, 47
Vocational rehabilitation counselor, 91, 100–102, 104, 122, 125
Vocational specialist, 125–126
Wellness counselor, 5
Youth counselor, 5, 91, 96–98, 104
Youth development aide, 97
Youth services worker, 97

NOTES

NOTES

NOTES

NOTES

DATE DUE

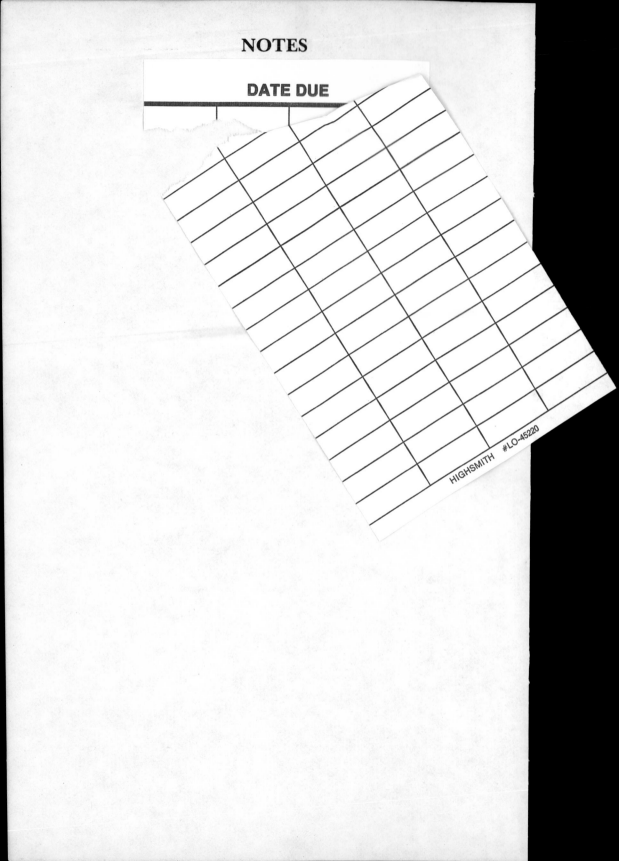

HIGHSMITH #LO-45220